All Kinds of Animals

A Beka Book® Pensacola, FL 32523-9100
an affiliate of PENSACOLA CHRISTIAN COLLEGE®

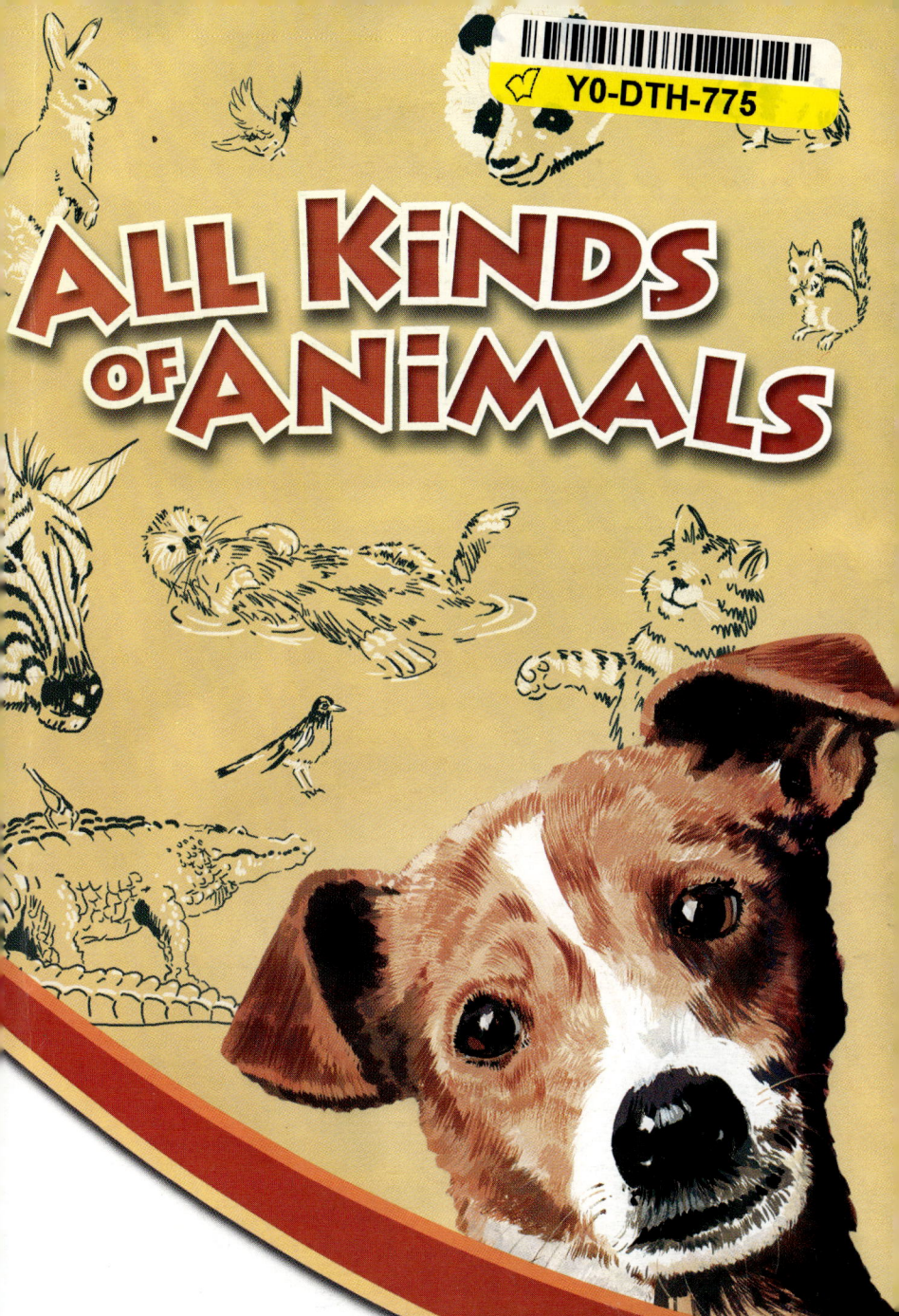

All Kinds of Animals
Third Edition

Staff Credits
Author: Judy Hull Moore
Editor: Laurel Hicks
Illustrators: Stan Shimmin, Ray Sanders
Designers: Tyler Nikkel, Thaddeus Lund

Copyright © mmvi, mcmlxxxviii, mcmlxxviii Pensacola Christian College
All rights reserved. Printed in U.S.A. 2015 C09

No part of this publication may be reproduced or transmitted in any form or by any means, electronic or mechanical, including photocopy, recording, or any information storage and retrieval system, or by license from any collective or licensing body, without permission in writing from the publisher.

A Beka Book, a Christian textbook ministry affiliated with Pensacola Christian College, is designed to meet the need for Christian textbooks and teaching aids. The purpose of this publishing ministry is to help Christian schools reach children and young people for the Lord and train them in the Christian way of life.

Cataloging Data

Moore, Judy Hull.
  All kinds of animals / Judy Hull Moore; edited
by Laurel Hicks.
  208 p.; col. ill.; 23 cm. + teacher's ed. (A Beka Book
reading program)
  For grade 2.
  1. Reading, Elementary. 2. Readers, Elementary.
III. Hicks, Laurel. IV. A Beka Book, Inc.
Library of Congress: PE119.M66 A5 2006
Dewey System: 428.6

Photo credits are listed left to right on a page. The abbreviation AA is used for Animals Animals Inc. Page 4—Henry Ausloos/AA, Robert Maier/AA; 5—Robert Pearcy/AA both; 8—Terence Gili/AA; 10—Jim Craigmyle/Corbis; 14—Dale Spartas/Corbis; 17—Julian Hoffman/AA; 18—DLILLC/Corbis; 20—J & B Photographers/AA; 23—Jorg & Petra Wegner/AA; 24—Robert Maier/AA; 25—Jerry Cooke/AA; 28—Sydney Thomson/AA; 32—DK Limited/Corbis; 33—Jerry Cooke/AA; 35—Lynn D. Odell/AA; 36—Hans Reinhard/zefa/Corbis; 39—Richard Kolar/AA; 41—Jorg & Petra Wegner/AA; 45—Jupiter Images, Corbis; 46—Ted Levin/AA; 49—Alan Carey/Photo Researchers, Inc.; 50—Joe McDonald/AA; 60—Corel; 64—Joe McDonald/Corbis; 66—Charles Palek/AA; 68—Leonard Lee Rue III/AA; 72—Peter Weimann/AA; 74—Zig Leszczynski/AA; 78—Zig Leszczynski/AA; 81—Joe McDonald/Corbis; 82—Zig Leszczynski/AA; 84—Zig Leszczynski/AA; 85—Zig Leszczynski/AA; 86—Tom & Pat Leeson/Photo Researchers, Inc.; 89—Gary W. Carter/Corbis; 91—Fred Unverham/AA; 92—Zig Leszczynski/AA; 93—Vicki Anderson/AA; 94—Breck P. Kent/AA; 95—George Godfrey/AA; 98—Corbis; 99—Bill Dyer/Photo Researchers, Inc., Phil Degginger/AA, John A. L. Cooke/AA; 102—William D. Griffin/AA; 108—Robert Lubeck/AA; 110—Bruce MacDonald/AA; 111—William D. Griffin/AA; 112—Breck P. Kent/AA; 114—C.W. Schwartz/AA; 118—F. E. Unverham/AA; 124—Ralph Reinhold/AA; 125—Alan G. Nelson/AA; 127—Alan & Sandy Carey/zefa/Corbis; 128—Tom Edwards/AA; 130—Jack Wilburn/AA; 134—Alan G. Nelson/AA; 137—Ralph Reinhold/AA; 140—Corbis; 141—Gerard Lacz/AA, Gerard Lacz/AA, Lynn Stone/AA; 142—Rich Reed/AA; 157—Brandon D. Cole/Corbis; 159—Corbis; 160—Fran Coleman/AA; 165—Fran Coleman/AA; 169—Fran Coleman/AA; 172—D. Allen Photography/AA; 174—Alain Dragesco-Joffe/AA; 176—Michel & Christine Denis-Huot/Photo Researchers Inc.; 177—Fran Coleman/AA; 180—Sunset Photo Agency/AA; 181—L.L.T. Rhodes/AA; 183—Fran Coleman/AA; 184—Grant Heilman/Grant Heilman Photography; 187—Corbis, William Ervin/Photo Researchers, Inc., Joe McDonald/AA; 190—Roger Tidman/Corbis; 195—Anthony Mercieca/AA; 200—Animals Animals; 203—Color-Pic/AA; 204—James J. Stachecki/AA.

CONTENTS

PETS ... 4
- Puppy Love ... 9
- Kittens ... 21
- Guinea Pigs ... 37

WOODLAND ANIMALS ... 45
- Cottontails ... 47
- Raccoons ... 65
- Chipmunks ... 83

GREAT AMERICAN SONGBIRDS ... 98
- Song Sparrow ... 103
- Cardinals ... 113
- Robins ... 125

ANIMALS FROM AROUND THE WORLD ... 140
- Sea Otters ... 143
- Giant Panda ... 161
- Largest Bird ... 173

AFRICAN PARTNERS ... 187
- Crocodile's Dentist ... 191
- Companions of the Ostrich ... 201

IN CONCLUSION ... 207

Pets

Almost every boy or girl in the world would like to have a pet. What kind of pet would you choose?

But wait! You will need to talk with your parents and brothers and sisters. You see, having a pet is a family affair. Did you say this is to be your very own pet and that you are going to take care of it yourself? That may be true when you are home, but what about when you are in school? And what if you spend the night at a friend's house? What if you come down with the flu or a bad cold? Who will take care of your pet then?

> **Words to watch for**
>
> **responsibility**—a job or duty
> **righteous**—being just or right
> **regard**—to look after or consider

Do you have a small brother or sister who could hurt your pet when you are not around? Sometimes a little child will hurt or scare an animal by playing too hard with it. Your pet may bite or scratch to protect itself and hurt your brother or sister.

Do you live in a small house or a big house? Is your house in town or on a farm? Where you live should help you decide if your pet will be large or small. Remember, a cute Saint Bernard puppy will grow into a huge dog in only one year. Large dogs need lots of space to run and to exercise. If you live in a small city apartment or in a house with a tiny yard, you will need a large place to exercise your dog every day.

Will you be one of the many people who treat pets like toys? You can play with toys for a while and then put them away and forget about them, but you can't go away and forget about your pet. Pets get hungry, just as you do. They need to be kept clean, just as you do. And just as you depend upon your mother and father, your pet will depend upon you!

Think about the questions you have just read. Then talk to your family about owning a pet.

Think of This!

Stop and think about all the different kinds of animals that God has created for us. Not only has He created animals that do important jobs for us, but He also has created animals just for us to love—pets! If you take the responsibility to love and care for one of God's creations, He will expect you to do your task well.

> **The Bible says**
> "A righteous man regardeth the life of his beast."
> —Proverbs 12:10

 Do You Remember?

Circle the correct answer.

1. Before you get a pet, you will need to talk with your parents and brothers and sisters about it.

    (Yes)   No

2. Pets are really just like toys.

    Yes   (No)

3. If you choose a pet, God expects you to take good care of that pet.

    (Yes)   No

4. A task is _____.

    (a) a job to do   (b) a game to play

Puppy Love

Starting Out Right

What is the most loyal pet a person could own? Most people would say, "A dog!" If their masters love and care for them, most dogs will love their masters so much that they would give their lives to protect them.

A dog seems to understand how its master feels. If you are happy, your dog will wiggle all over with delight. If you are sad, his eyes seem to tell you that he understands.

You may wish to have such a faithful dog-friend right now. But wait! Most dogs have grown up to love and obey *another* master, and it is hard to teach a grown dog new ways. What you probably should have is a puppy, about eight weeks old, instead

---
Words to watch for

loyal—faithful   **master**—owner

Puppy Love

of a full-grown dog. Then if you are kind to him, your puppy will grow up to love and trust *you*.

Perhaps the most exciting day in your puppy's life is the day you become his master. But you must remember—an eight-week-old puppy that has just been taken from his mother is very frightened.

Before you bring him home, make a bed for your puppy. An old playpen is a good place. Cover the floor of the pen, or a large

box, with newspaper. Then, when you bring him home, let him sniff and explore his home. This will be his special place until he grows a little bigger. While he is exploring, pat him and talk softly to him.

The first night, give him a few tablespoons of warm milk. The next morning you may give him some warm baby cereal mixed with milk. (His food should never be hot.)

— Puppy Love

When it is time for you to go to bed, wrap a filled hot water bottle in a soft cloth. Then wrap a ticking alarm clock in another cloth. (Be sure the alarm clock is not set to go off!) Place these in the pen or box with the puppy. It may sound funny, but the warmth of the hot water bottle and the ticking sound of the clock will remind the

puppy of his mother. He will not be as frightened when he is left alone.

If your puppy does cry when you leave the room, gently but firmly say "No!" and then leave. You may be sad to hear his cries, but you are his master. If you give in to him tonight, he will expect you to give in the next night. Then your parents will be unhappy. The first night home is the time you begin to train your puppy. When your puppy knows what to expect from you, he will be content in your home.

If you choose a puppy that will grow to be a large dog, handle him as much as possible during the first two months while he is still small. Hold him in your arms. Gently take things out of his mouth. Never allow him to nip you, even when you are playing. You are training him to trust and obey you when he is older and much bigger.

Puppy Love

By now you have probably chosen a name for your puppy. Call him by name often. Soon he should come when you call. If he will not come to you after he knows his name, do not chase after him. He will think the chase is a great game. Then every time you call him, he will lead you on a merry chase! Instead, kneel to the floor. Tap your fingers on the floor and firmly say, "Come!"

Do You Remember?

Circle the correct answer.

1. If you want a loving, loyal pet, it is best to get _____.

    (a) a full-grown dog   (b) a puppy

2. If your puppy cries when you leave him at night, let him sleep with you.

    Yes   No

3. Something that makes a good bed for your puppy is _____.

    (a) a playpen   (b) a hot water bottle

4. If your puppy doesn't come when you call, chase him.

    Yes   No

5. A puppy that is content is _____.

    (a) worried   (b) happy   (c) sad

15

Puppy Love

Making Your Puppy Obey

As the weeks go by, you can be sure there will be times when your puppy disobeys you. What should you do?

First, be sure he understands what you have asked him to do. As soon as he begins to do something bad, say "No" in a gentle, firm voice. No one likes to be yelled at, not even dogs.

If he continues to disobey you, roll a newspaper to look like a log. Slap it against your hand, making a loud sound, and say "No!" again. If he still does not stop, take hold of his collar with one hand, and with the rolled-up newspaper in the other hand, slap his hind legs. The newspaper will make a loud sound that will scare him, but it will not hurt him.

Above all, make sure your puppy obeys you every time. When he does obey you, tell him how happy you are. Pat him. Give him a treat. Knowing he has made you happy makes him happy, too. Then he will be eager to please you the next time.

Yes, it is a big day for both you and your puppy when you become his owner. As the days go by, you both will mean more to each other. Your puppy will trust you to meet his every need.

Puppy Love

Think of This!

Do you want your puppy to be a loyal friend? Then be a loyal master. Be fair to your pet just as you want your friends to be fair with you.

The Bible says

"A man that hath friends must shew himself friendly."   —Proverbs 18:24

Do You Remember?

Circle the correct answer.

1. When your puppy *continues* to disobey, he _____.

    (a) disobeys once and stops

    (b) keeps on disobeying over and over

2. If your dog disobeys, you should first roll up a newspaper.

    Yes   No

3. What will make your dog glad to obey you?

    (a) getting spanked

    (b) getting a pat and a treat

    (c) being ignored when he does right

 What Do You Think?

1. Why is it important to train your puppy to obey?

2. Why is it important for your parents to teach you to obey?

Kittens

Choosing a Kitten

This is the day Jenny has been waiting for for many weeks. Six weeks ago, her friend's cat had kittens. When Jenny asked her parents if they would let her have a kitten, they said "Yes."

Now, wide-eyed Jenny looked over the four fat, furry kittens. Four wide-eyed kittens looked right back at Jenny. She wiggled her finger over the kittens' box. The gray and white kitten batted its paw at her.

"That one!" cried Jenny. "She is so pretty and soft. Why, that's what I'll name her—Pretty!"

Words to watch for

stalking—creeping up on

— Kittens

Jenny carefully lifted Pretty out of her box and took her to the car. She put Pretty into a small cardboard box for the ride home. The ride scared the small kitten. Suddenly she felt all alone. "Meow, meow!" she cried.

 Do You Remember?
Circle the correct answer.

1. What did Jenny's kitten do when Jenny wiggled her finger over the kittens?

    (a) meow   (b) batted her finger

2. Why did the kitten "meow" on the ride home?

    (a) she wanted food

    (b) she was afraid

    (c) she was glad to leave her mother

3. What name did Jenny give her kitten?

    (a) Snowflake   (b) Pretty   (c) Kitty

Baby Kittens

As soon as they were home, Jenny lined a cardboard box with newspapers. Then she padded it with soft rags. Pretty curled up to take a nap. Young kittens sleep most of the day, so Jenny could not hold her kitten often.

Jenny should feed her kitten four small meals a day. She should also give her kitten plenty of warm milk and fresh water. What else should Jenny know about her kitten? Let's find out.

KITTENS

When kittens are born, their eyes are closed. Because of this, we say newborn kittens are blind. They are helpless and cannot even purr! The mother stays close beside her kittens. She hardly leaves them at all. As she washes them with her rough, pink tongue, she lets them drink her warm milk. They listen to her happy purr as she takes care of them.

When the kittens are about a week old, they purr for the very first time. After the kittens are eight, nine, or ten days old, their eyes open and they see their mother for the very first time. They are very content and happy.

When they are two weeks old, the kittens start walking around on very shaky legs. And when they are three weeks old, they begin to play with each other.

Kittens

 Do You Remember?

Circle the correct answer.

1. Jenny can't hold her kitten as much as she wants because _____.

    (a) the kitten could be easily hurt

    (b) Pretty sleeps most of the day

2. A newborn kitten cannot see because _____.

    (a) it is really blind

    (b) its eyes do not open for eight to ten days

3. Kittens walk for the first time when they are about _____.

    (a) two weeks old

    (b) three weeks old

    (c) ten days old

A Kitten's Play

The games that kittens play are very important. Have you ever wondered why a mother cat will let her kittens pounce on her tail as she wags it back and forth? She probably knows she is training them how to pounce on mice and other small animals.

Jenny does not know it, but when she ties a piece of paper to the end of a string and lets Pretty bat it back and forth, she is training her kitten how to catch low-flying moths and other insects. When Pretty is older, Jenny will see Pretty leap ten feet to pounce upon an insect in the grass. And she will hardly ever miss her target!

As Pretty gets older, Jenny will find that if she makes a scratching sound against her kitten's box, Pretty will come stalking as if to pounce. Why? Pretty is pretending to

Kittens

play "cat and mouse." You see, mice and rats make a scratching sound, and Pretty is pretending to catch one. This reminds Jenny of how she plays "cops and robbers" with her brother!

Cats are very clean pets. Since cats are always washing themselves, Jenny will never need to give her cat a bath unless Pretty falls into something very dirty.

Cats are also very graceful. Jenny will be amazed to see Pretty walk across a crowded toy shelf without knocking a single toy off!

When the flower garden blooms in spring, how Jenny will laugh to see Pretty sniffing the flowers and the catnip! Cats cannot smell as well as dogs, but they do love sweet smells!

KITTENS

 Do You Remember?

Circle the correct answer.

1. Playing with their mother's tail trains the kittens to _____ .

    (a) catch insects   (**b**) pounce on mice

2. Jenny helps train her cat to catch moths and other insects by letting her bat at paper tied to a string.

    (Yes)   No

3. A scratching sound reminds a kitten of _____ .

    (a) her mother   (**b**) a mouse   (c) an insect

4. Circle the words which best tell what a cat does.

    (**a**) pounces   (**b**) stalks   (c) hops

    (**d**) plays   (e) gnaws   (**f**) leaps

30

A Cat's Way of Life

As Pretty grows older, Jenny will learn that she cannot expect her cat to obey her the way her brother's dog obeys him. Even though they may love their owner very much, cats have a mind of their own.

There is a big oak tree in the garden that Pretty loves to scratch on. Jenny's father tells her that a cat's claws are always growing, just as our fingernails are. We cut our fingernails when they are too long, but cats must wear their claws down by scratching on trees and other rough things. This also keeps their claws clean.

Jenny's parents are wise. They have made a special scratching post from twine and a piece of old carpet. They keep this scratching

> **Words to watch for**
>
> **sacrifice**—to give up something that is loved

Kittens

post inside the house beside Pretty's box so she will not scratch the furniture.

A day will come when Pretty will begin to catch birds and other small animals. Jenny will scold her cat, but it will not make much difference to Pretty. It would be useless to spank Pretty, for she would not understand.

Catching small animals is part of God's plan for cats. If some birds and other small animals were not caught, there would be too many of these animals. They would starve because there would not be enough food for all of them. And think of the diseases that would spread if mice and rats were not killed by cats!

One morning Pretty will catch a mouse. Instead of eating it, she will pick it up and

 **Kittens**

lay it at Jenny's feet as a gift. This may not seem like much of a gift to Jenny, but to Pretty, giving up the mouse is a big sacrifice. This is just a cat's way of saying, "Thank you for taking good care of me. I think you are pretty special!"

 Do You Remember?
Circle the correct answer.

1. Cats scratch on trees and other things _____.

    (a) to wear down their claws

    (b) to practice climbing

    (c) to find insects to catch

2. Catching birds and small animals is part of God's plan for a cat.

       No

Word Practice

Can you divide these compound words?

newborn   cardboard

fingernails   catnip

What Do You Think?

1. Why is it important for kittens to play?

2. What do cats do that some people don't like? Why do they do these things? Is it wrong?

Guinea Pigs

What Is a Guinea Pig?

Many children have learned that the guinea pig makes a delightful pet. Guinea pigs are very gentle and will hardly ever bite or scratch unless they are badly frightened. They are also easy to raise and care for.

After a guinea pig has been in your home for a while, it will learn to recognize its human friends. At meal times it will make little squeals and whistles when you enter the room. Although this may sound somewhat like a pig's squeals, don't be fooled. The guinea pig is not a kind of pig but a rodent.

Rodents are animals that gnaw. They have two very sharp front teeth that never stop growing as long as they live. For this

> **Words to watch for**
>
> **gnaw**—to chew on something

Guinea Pigs

reason, all rodents need to wear their teeth down by gnawing. Guinea pigs, chipmunks, squirrels, beavers, rats, and mice are all rodents.

The guinea pig has not always lived in the United States. Guinea pigs came from Central and South America. There the Inca Indians raised them for pets and for food.

Do You Remember?

Circle the correct answer.

1. A guinea pig is really a kind of
   _____.

    (a) dog   (b) rodent   (c) pig

2. A rodent is an animal that _____.

    (a) digs   (b) gnaws   (c) flies

3. *Gnaw* means _____.

    (a) to chew

    (b) to eat

    (c) to sleep all winter

What Do Guinea Pigs Look Like?

Guinea pigs have pointed, whiskered faces. They scurry along on short legs and little feet. And guinea pigs have very short tails—so short that even their short hair hides them.

Usually guinea pigs have short hair, but some kinds have long hair. Short-haired guinea pigs are much easier to care for as pets. Most guinea pigs are grey or black or

Guinea Pigs

a reddish brown. But no matter what color they are, they usually have patches of white hair.

Baby guinea pigs are very cute. Unlike most other rodents, they are born with all their hair. Their eyes are open, and in only a few days they are nibbling at their parents' food.

Do You Remember?
Circle the correct answer.

1. Guinea pigs have pointed faces and _____.

   (a) tall, thin bodies

   (b) short legs with little feet

   (c) long legs with big feet

2. *Patches* of white hair means the same as _____.

   (a) spots   (b) stripes

3. Guinea pigs, like cats are born blind.

   Yes   No

What to Feed Guinea Pigs

Guinea pigs enjoy almost all uncooked vegetables such as cabbage, lettuce leaves, and carrots. They like the green tops of beets and carrots that most people throw away. Guinea pigs also need hay and dry feed that is made of a mixture of grains. The dry feed can be bought at a pet store.

Guinea Pigs

Hay is more difficult to get unless you live on or near a farm. If you cannot get hay, go to a farm-feed store or pet shop and ask for the rabbit pellets that contain hay as well as grain.

A small block of rock salt should be kept in your pet's cage. If you cannot get this at your pet store, sprinkle table salt over your pet's food twice a week.

And, of course, your guinea pig needs fresh water every day. Don't make the mistake of putting a dish or a pan of water into the cage. If your guinea pig does not upset it, he will scratch and kick dirt into it. Then he won't drink it, and you will have a mess of splashed water to clean up. Instead, buy a special water bottle for guinea pigs in your pet store.

If you want to have a healthy, happy guinea pig for a pet, here are five things to do:

1. Feed it twice a day. After five or ten minutes, remove any uneaten food. This will keep your pet's cage clean.

2. Clean the cage twice a week. Remove old newspaper and put fresh paper down. Wash the cage once a week. Then keep the cage dry. A wet cage will make your pet sick.

3. Give your pet fresh drinking water every day.

4. Keep a small block of rock salt in its cage.

5. Keep your guinea pig's cage inside the house where the temperature never goes below 65°.

Guinea Pigs

🐾 Do You Remember?

Circle the correct answer.

1. Circle the foods guinea pigs like or need to eat.

    (a) hamburger (b) bread (c) lettuce

    (d) grain (e) milk (f) water

    (g) carrots (h) hay (i) meat bones

    (j) rock salt

2. For a guinea pig's water, you should buy a special _____.

    (a) dish (b) rabbit pellet

    (c) water bottle

3. Guinea pigs may be kept outdoors all year round.

    Yes   No

🐾 What Do You Think?

1. What things must a guinea pig trust his owner to do for him?

2. What things do you need to trust God to do for you?

WOODLAND ANIMALS

Have you ever taken a walk through the woods? Perhaps you thought, "My, what a quiet place!" Maybe all you could hear were leaves crunching under your feet.

The forest may seem very quiet, but it is a very busy place. Chipmunks and squirrels scamper back and forth with their precious nuts. Mother animals teach their babies how to do things for themselves. Large animals hunt for smaller animals. Small animals watch and hide from large animals.

You may not have seen a creature on your walk through the woods, but be sure of this—some woodland creature has seen you!

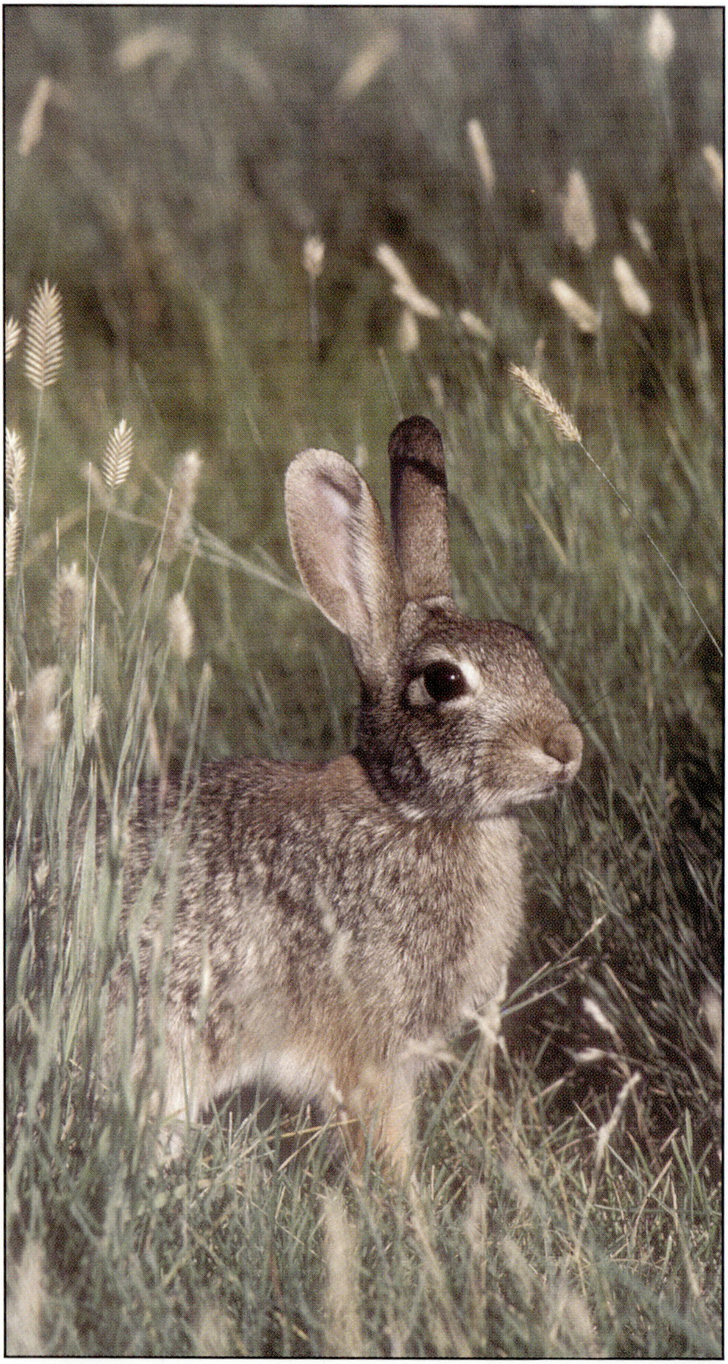

COTTONTAILS

Resting and Watching

The sun was beginning to set in the meadow near the woodland. Mrs. Cottontail's dark eyes opened. She saw a tiny field mouse scurry through the clover. Nearby a butterfly landed on a buttercup. Mrs. Cottontail blinked her eyes and wiggled her nose as she looked at the wild raspberry bush growing near the edge of the woods. She needed to keep her eyes on that bush.

At dawn, she had chosen a patch of tall grass and weeds to hide in for the day. It was not far from the raspberry bush. All day long she had dozed for only a few minutes at a time. She had hardly moved except to wiggle her nose or twitch her whiskers. She hadn't even wiggled her ears!

Words to watch for
raspberry

COTTONTAILS

She looked again at the raspberry bush. It was not dark yet, so she closed her eyes again. She sat so still that her brown fur looked like part of the tall grass. No enemy must find her or she would become their dinner. Then who would watch the wild raspberry bush?

Soon it was dark. Yellow moonlight shone over the meadow. Mrs. Cottontail gave three short hops and then sat up on her hind legs to look around. She sniffed the air. The meadow seemed safe. Still she had to be careful. The owls that fly at night like rabbit dinners, too.

Mrs. Cottontail took a few nibbles of sweet clover. She got a drink by licking the dew from some clover leaves. Then she quickly hopped over to the bush she had been watching all day. Making sure nothing was watching her, she crawled under the raspberry bush. With her teeth, she pulled a soft fur blanket off a fur-lined nest. Inside the nest were four pink-skinned bunnies.

The bunnies were only one day old and did not look very much like rabbits. Their fuzzy fur was just beginning to grow. They could neither see nor hear. There were only lines where their eyes would be. And their ears lay back flat against their heads.

baby bunnies in fur-lined nest

COTTONTAILS

Mrs. Cottontail knew that one week from now they would look very different. Their dark eyes would be open. Their ears would stand up straight and they would be able to hear. They would be soft and furry like her.

The baby cottontails needed their mother, but she could come to them only at night. She was not being lazy or mean. She knew that if she came during the day, she might lead an enemy to the babies' nest.

🐾 Do You Remember?

Circle the correct answer.

1. Mrs. Cottontail watched the raspberry bush because _____.

    (a) an enemy was in the bush

    (b) her babies were in a nest there

2. For a drink, Mrs. Cottontail _____.

    (a) licked dew from a leaf

    (b) found a small stream of water

3. The mother rabbit knew that if she came to the nest in the daytime, an enemy might find her babies.

        Yes   No

Word Practice

Divide these compound words.

    w o o d l a n d   c o t t o n t a i l

    n e a r b y   b u t t e r c u p

    m o o n l i g h t   a n y m o r e

Building a Nest

Before her babies were born, Mrs. Cottontail chose a safe place under a raspberry bush to build her nest. First, she dug a hole the size of a small bowl. With her teeth she began pulling fur from her body. Mixing her fur with grass, she lined the hole she had dug. When she finished, her nest was nice and soft.

Like all good mothers, she wanted to be able to protect her babies and keep them warm. So next she made a blanket by pulling out more of her fur and mixing it with grass. She placed this blanket over the nest and scattered leaves over the top of it. Her nest was finished. Just by looking at it, you could not tell a nest was there. It looked just like part of the ground around it.

Taking Care of Her Family

Now, Mrs. Cottontail snuggled down close to her babies. She gave them a meal of nice warm milk. When her babies were full and sleepy, Mrs. Cottontail pulled the warm blanket back over her babies and hopped away. The blanket would not only keep them warm, but it would also keep an enemy from seeing the nest.

COTTONTAILS

Many times that night, she went to the nest. She fed her babies warm milk. She washed them with her pink tongue and combed their new baby hair with her claws. Each time she left to nibble on clover, she carefully pulled the blanket back over the nest. Her babies were well hidden.

The night was the only safe time for Mrs. Cottontail to eat. During the day there were too many weasels, hawks, snakes, and foxes moving around in the forest. A smart cottontail stays hidden during the day unless something tries to harm her young family.

Dawn came. She knew she must leave her babies for the day. She had to find a hiding place in which to rest until night. Then she would return to her family.

🐾 Do You Remember?
Write the correct answer in the blank.

1. Mrs. Cottontail made her babies' blanket out of grass and

   _____.

2. Mother Cottontail works in the night and rests in the

   _____.

COTTONTAILS

Word Practice

1. Divide these words into syllables.

   n i b b l e   m o o n l i g h t

   c o t t o n t a i l

2. Two of the above words are compound words. Circle them.

What Are "Forms"?

Mother rabbits build nests only for their babies. Grown rabbits do not live in nests. Each day they choose a different resting spot that will protect them from their enemies and from the weather. We call this place the rabbit's *form*.

If it is a hot day, the form may be in a hollow log or in the shade of a cool rock. On a rainy day, the rabbit may choose to be under a bush or under the edge of a rock to keep dry.

Danger!

The warm spring day passed slowly as Mrs. Cottontail napped and watched the raspberry bush from a clump of buttercups. In the afternoon she heard a movement in the grass. Her nose twitched. She smelled danger, but she dared not move.

Near the bush she saw a weasel. She knew a hungry weasel could easily eat all four of her babies. If she had to, she would risk her own life to save her babies.

Mrs. Cottontail had tricks she could use on Mr. Weasel. She could run right in front of him. Then Mr. Weasel would forget about the nest and chase her. But weasels are faster than rabbits, and Mrs. Cottontail would probably be caught. If the weasel or any other animal kept after the nest instead of chasing her, she could use her sharp hind claws to kick and scratch.

COTTONTAILS

The weasel came closer to her hidden nest. Just as she was ready to jump from her form, she heard a loud bang that scared her even more than seeing the weasel. As she crouched in the grass, she heard the footsteps. A farmer walked over to pick up the dead weasel he had just shot. He seemed very happy to get the animal that had been bothering his chickens. Mrs. Cottontail was very lucky. Weasels are much faster and stronger than rabbits.

🐾 Do You Remember?

Circle the correct answer.

1. A form is the place where _____.

    (a) the baby rabbits' nest is

    (b) Mrs. Cottontail rests during the day

2. Mrs. Cottontail could probably save her babies _____.

    (a) by making a loud noise to scare the enemy

    (b) by destroying her enemy's nest

    (c) by getting the enemy to chase her

3. The _____ saved the baby rabbits.

    (a) weasel

    (b) mother cottontail

    (c) farmer

COTTONTAILS

Growing Up

When the cottontail bunnies are about two months old, they will be completely on their own. By winter their fur will be thick. Each young cottontail will make his own form under the edge of a rock or under a bush. From there he will watch the snow fall. Since there are no green plants to eat during the winter, he must eat twigs and the bark from small fruit trees and bushes.

What a sweet smell spring brings to the woods and meadow! Now there are green plants to eat again. The rabbits no longer think of their mother nor of their brothers or sisters. Only a year old, each rabbit is fully grown and ready to begin its own family.

COTTONTAILS

Think of This!

The mother cottontail will give her life to protect her babies. Does this make you think of Someone Who gave His life for you to save you from your sins?

The Bible says

"Christ died for our sins." —1 Corinthians 15:3

Do You Remember?

Circle the correct answer.

1. The young cottontails will be completely on their own when they are _____.

    (a) about two months old

    (b) about two weeks old

    (c) about two days old

2. In winter, cottontails eat _____.

   (a) green plants

   (b) snow

   (c) twigs and bark

3. A cottontail is old enough to start its own family when it is _____.

   (a) 12 months old

   (b) four months old

   (c) six months old

What Do You Think?

1. Is the mother cottontail a good mother? Why?

2. In what special ways has God provided protection for young cottontails?

3. In what ways has God provided protection for you?

63

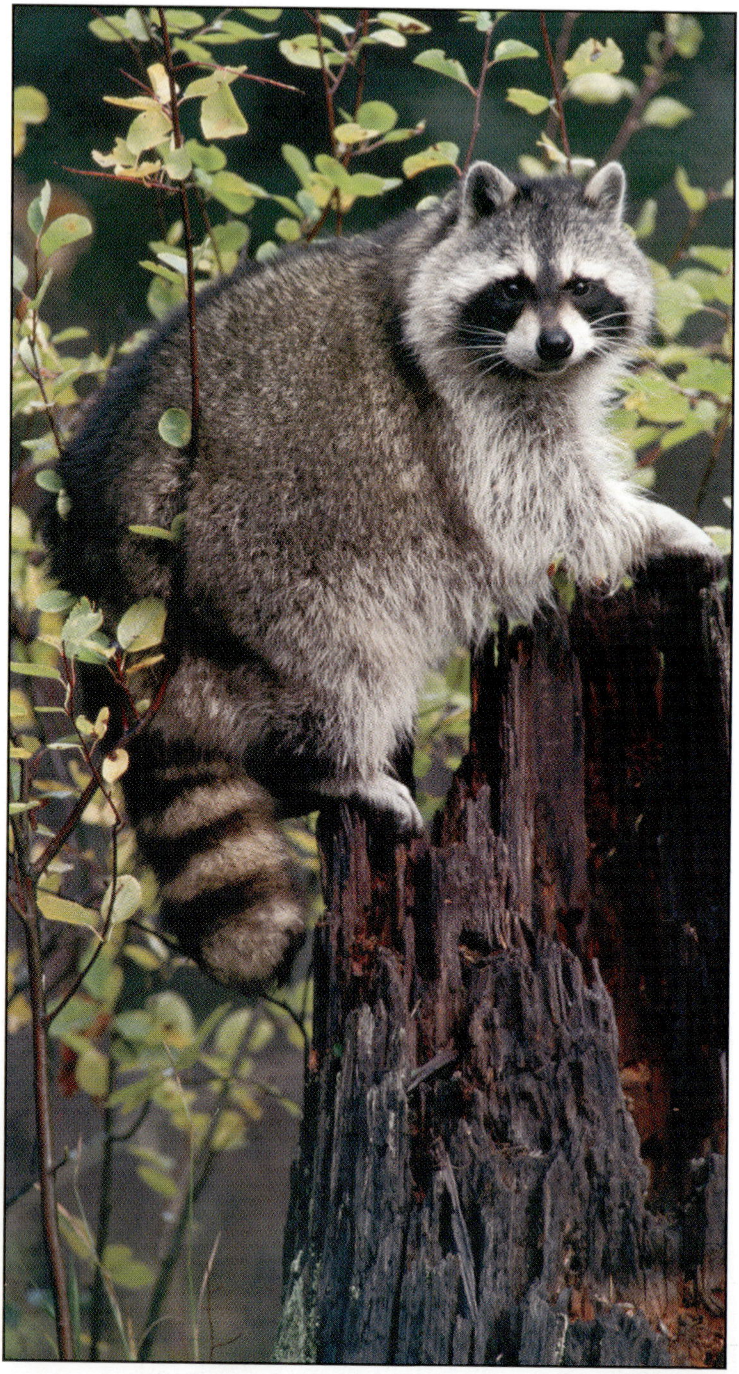

RACCOONS

Nighttime in the Woods

Night is falling in the country. In a nearby woods, animals of the day are getting ready for a good night's rest. Birds are settling down in their nests with their young. A fox turns round and round and then lies down—his fluffy red tail over his nose. The shy little chipmunk runs down its burrow and curls up on a bed of leaves.

But not all animals of the forest go to sleep at night. Some are just waking up. The screech owl blinks his eyes as he scans the ground below for a mouse or any other small animal that would make a fine meal. "Who-oo-o," he calls through the still night. The moon rises higher. An opossum climbs over a tree's branches in search of a bird nest where he hopes to find his dinner.

Words to watch for

scan—to look around
kit—a baby animal that has fur

Raccoons

Nearby is a large, dead tree. Several rotten branches have fallen from it. It was easy for an animal to dig out a hole in the rotting trunk for a den. Now a furry, black-masked "robber" has found the hole and scooped it out to make a bigger house.

Who is this "furry, black-masked robber"? It's really a raccoon! The wide, black stripe of fur that goes around his eyes and across his cheeks makes us think of a robber's mask. The raccoon's coat is made of long white, black, and gray hair. Around his tail are five to seven black rings of fur.

RACCOONS

🐾 Do You Remember?

Circle the correct answer.

1. A den is an animal's _____.

    (a) playground

    (b) house

    (c) food

2. Which makes the raccoon look like a robber? _____.

    (a) the rings around his tail

    (b) the bands of black fur around his eyes

    (c) his fur coat

Learning to Obey

Do you hear a sound coming from inside the hole in the tree? Mrs. Raccoon has just left. What could the noise be?

Inside the tree are three furry kits. *Kits* is another name for baby raccoons. The kits are young enough to be timid of the huge world that surrounds their small tree home. Yet they are old enough to be curious.

Playfully, the three kits roll over each other in their warm den. From time to time, they stop their play, and peek out of the "door" of their home.

They all seem to agree that it is a long way down to the bottom of the tree. Not one of them knows if they should climb down head first or tail first.

Raccoons

Suddenly, they hear growls and hisses. The three kits flatten their ears against their heads. How ashamed they look as they pull their heads back inside their den. Mother raccoon has been watching them from the ground below. She seems to know her kits' thoughts. She warns her young to stay in their safe den until she returns with their dinner. You can be sure that she has promised a punishment for any of her kits that disobeys.

Why is Mrs. Raccoon so strict? She knows that a screech owl lives in the forest. It is night and he is searching for his dinner, too. A young raccoon is not too heavy for a screech owl to carry away.

Knowing that her kits have obeyed her, she disappears into the darkness of the night. She will begin her nightly search for food.

🐾 Do You Remember?

Circle the correct answer.

1. Mother raccoon wanted her kits to stay in the den because _____.

    (a) an enemy might carry them away

    (b) they might fall out of the tree

    (c) they might drown in the stream

2. How did the mother warn her kits to stay in their den?

    (a) by biting them

    (b) by growling and hissing

    (c) by nudging them back inside the den

3. Both the screech owl and the raccoon hunt _____.

    (a) in the morning

    (b) in the afternoon

    (c) in the night

Raccoons

Supper's Ready!

Nearby is a wide stream. Raccoons love to make their homes near water. They are able to find plenty of good food in or near the stream. Fish, crayfish, and frogs are a raccoon's delight.

Mrs. Raccoon sticks her paw into the water and overturns small rocks. Raccoons use their front paws like we use our hands. They are even able to untie knots and turn door knobs with the fingers of their front paws. They also have very sharp claws. So it is easy for Mrs. Raccoon to turn over stones.

Tonight Mrs. Raccoon finds a crayfish. With both paws, she cracks it open; then she swishes it up and down in the water. Most raccoons like to "dunk" their food in water. Food is easier for them to swallow when it is wet.

Raccoons

Not too far away from the stream she begins to dig in the sand. Before long she uncovers turtle eggs. What a feast she has! Back at the stream she is able to sneak up on a frog which becomes part of her dinner, too.

At last her stomach is full. She begins to think about what she can take back to her youngsters. She puts her paw back into the stream. Quickly she catches a rather large fish. Carrying the fish in her mouth, she starts back to her family.

She knows that soon she will need to bring her three kits with her. They are getting too big to keep in the tree much longer. They have many lessons to learn from their wise mother before the cold winter comes.

RACCOONS

🐾 Do You Remember?
Write the correct answer in the blank.

1. Raccoons can use their front paws the way we use our

   _____.

2. What did Mrs. Raccoon take back to feed her kits?

   _____.

Things to Learn

Young raccoons must learn how to hide and escape from their enemies. They must learn where to find food such as earthworms, turtle and bird eggs, and fruit. They must also learn how to catch mice, insects, and birds as well as food in the stream.

By the time winter comes, raccoons must be fat and furry or they will starve. There is not much food to be found in the winter when the stream is frozen over. Because of this, raccoons find a place to curl up and sleep through most of the cold days of winter. They eat and eat and become fatter and fatter during the summer and fall. In the winter, the fat they have stored keeps them warm and keeps them from starving. Only on sunny winter days will a raccoon leave its den to hunt for food.

Raccoons

But for now, Mrs. Raccoon watches her kits play with the fish before they eat it. Then after they finish eating, the kits nip each other and roll over their mother in play.

Through the hole of the tree come the first rays of sunrise. Three sleepy raccoons curl up with their tired mother to sleep out the day. As the mother raccoon licks her kits' soft fur, she thinks about where she will hunt tonight. At last asleep, she dreams of a corn field she has seen on a nearby farm. Sweet, juicy corn!

Think of This!

The mother raccoon showed her love for her kits by training them to obey her even if it meant punishing them. She was a wise mother and could teach them many things. But she could teach them only if they obeyed. Your parents have important things to teach you, too. Do you obey them?

The Bible says

"Children, obey your parents in the Lord: for this is right." —*Ephesians 6:1*

RACCOONS

🐾 Do You Remember?

Circle the correct answer. Each will have two or more answers.

1. Young raccoons must learn how to
   _____.

   (a) catch food   (b) sleep

   (c) hide from enemies

2. It is hard for raccoons to find food in the winter because_____.

   (a) it is too cold to go out looking

   (b) the streams freeze over

   (c) the plants die

3. Raccoons eat _____.

   (a) turtle eggs   (b) fish   (c) worms

   (d) mice   (e) spinach   (f) insects

   (g) corn   (h) bark   (i) acorns

   (j) frogs

What Do You Think?

The mother raccoon seemed to know what her kits were thinking. Instead of leaving to find food, she stayed beneath the tree. She was checking to see that her kits stayed where they belonged.

1. Do you think the mother raccoon was wise? Why?
2. Do you think it's a good idea for your mother to check on you? Should she have to check on you very often? Why?
3. In what ways is the raccoon a good mother?

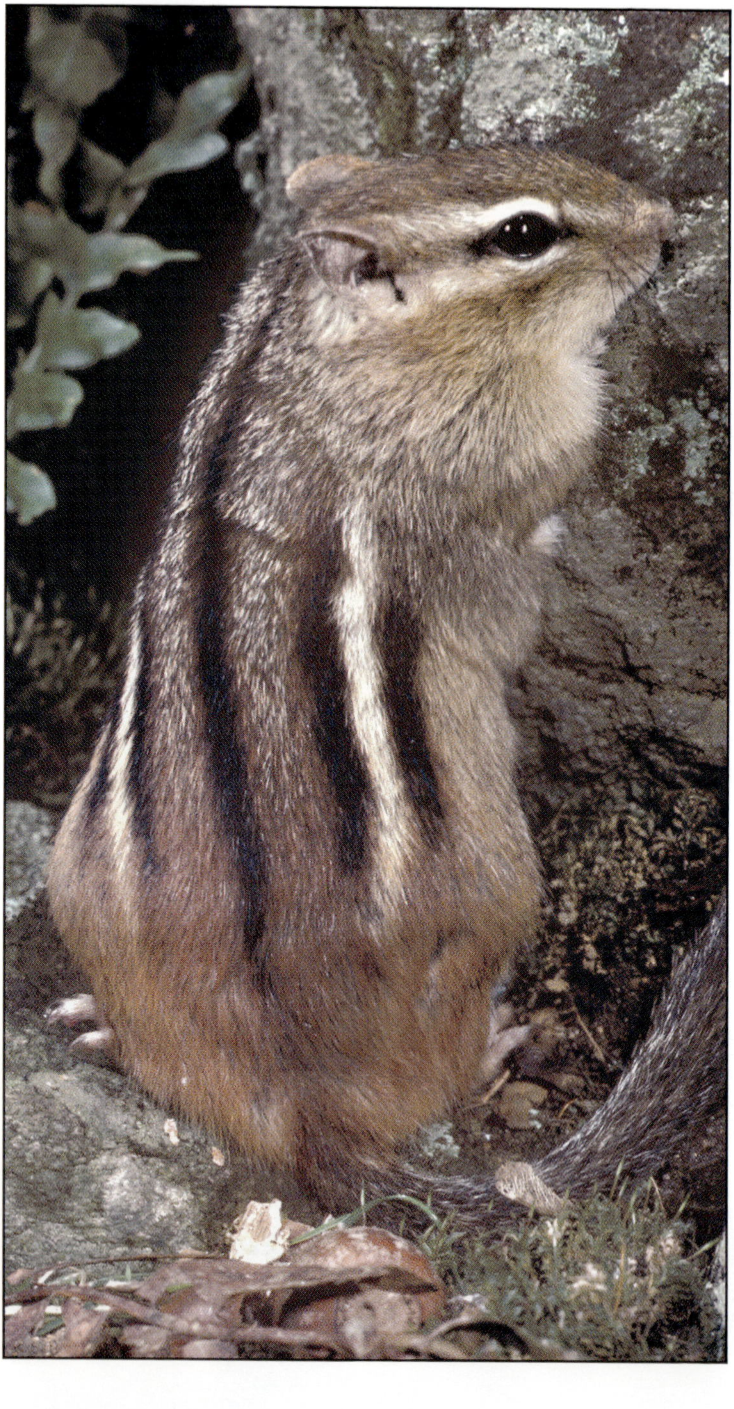

CHIPMUNKS

Meet a Chippie

Have you ever been on an autumn picnic near a woods? If you have, perhaps you have seen a small, brown, furry animal skittering back and forth across the fallen leaves. Maybe you thought the busy little creature had the mumps because its cheeks bulged so!

And you probably said, "Look, Mom! There's a squirrel!"

But if you look closely, you can see that this creature couldn't be a squirrel. Squirrels do not have black and tan stripes around their eyes and down their backs; this animal does. Its tail is furry, but thin, not at all bushy like a squirrel's tail. In fact, its whole body is much smaller than a

> **Words to watch for**
> **burrow**—an animal's home in the ground
> **kernels**—seeds

CHIPMUNKS

squirrel's. Many people call this small animal a "chippie," but it is really a chipmunk.

A chipmunk is a harmless rodent. Most people think only of rats and mice when they hear someone speak of rodents. Rodents are a group of animals that include chipmunks, squirrels, beavers, hamsters, mice, rats, and some other animals. So you see, some rodents are quite harmless. You may even know of someone who has a rodent for a pet. Remember the guinea pig?

All rodents are gnawing animals. And each kind of rodent has something special it likes to gnaw on. A chipmunk's favorite food is nuts. How does a chipmunk crack them open? God gave each chipmunk a set of nutcrackers—four very sharp front teeth! Biting nut shells wears the chipmunk's teeth down, but they never get too short, because their teeth keep growing all the time.

CHIPMUNKS

🐾 Do You Remember?

Circle the correct answer.

1. A chipmunk belongs to a group of animals called _____.

    (a) squirrels   (b) rodents   (c) chippies

2. Circle the things that make a chipmunk different from a squirrel.

    (a) stripes   (b) thin, furry tail
    (c) teeth   (d) bushy tail
    (e) smaller size

3. A chipmunk's favorite food is _____.

    (a) nuts   (b) fish   (c) bark

Preparing for Winter

You may wonder why the chipmunk scampers around so. Did you see him stuff something into his mouth? He is looking for nuts and seeds to store away in his burrow for the cold winter months ahead.

It may surprise you to know that in Chippie's burrow or tunnel, he has dug out several small rooms. One is his bedroom. The others are storerooms. In the summer Chippie begins filling each storeroom for winter. Although he loves fruit and berries, he is smart enough to know that they would rot and spoil the other food he has stored. Then he would starve. So he is careful to choose only dry seeds and nuts.

When Chippie gets his storerooms full, he begins to fill his bedroom. Did you know

CHIPMUNKS

that a chipmunk always has a bed in his bedroom? His bed is made of dry leaves. Where does he put the nuts? Why, every bed needs a mattress! The chipmunk's mattress is made of stored nuts and seeds. There he will store about a bushel in all.

Think how big a bushel basket is. Now think how big a chipmunk is. How does such a tiny animal store so much? Remember how the chipmunk's cheeks bulged so? You may have thought he had the mumps, but he really had a mouth full of seeds.

CHIPMUNKS

God has carefully designed each animal so that it can do a certain job. On each side of a chipmunk's mouth there is a pouch. When the chipmunk finds an acorn, he nips off the sharp ends of the nut that might cut his mouth. Then he stuffs the acorn into one of his cheek pouches. The next nut he finds he puts into the other pouch. He always keeps the same number of nuts in each pouch. He keeps this up until he has four acorns in each pouch. If he finds still another acorn, he will put it between his front teeth. (Can you figure out how many acorns that makes?) Then off he scampers to his burrow. Sometimes his cheeks bulge so much that he cannot get through the tiny doorway to his burrow. Then he must turn his head sideways to get through!

Have you figured out how many acorns a chipmunk can carry at one time? Nine

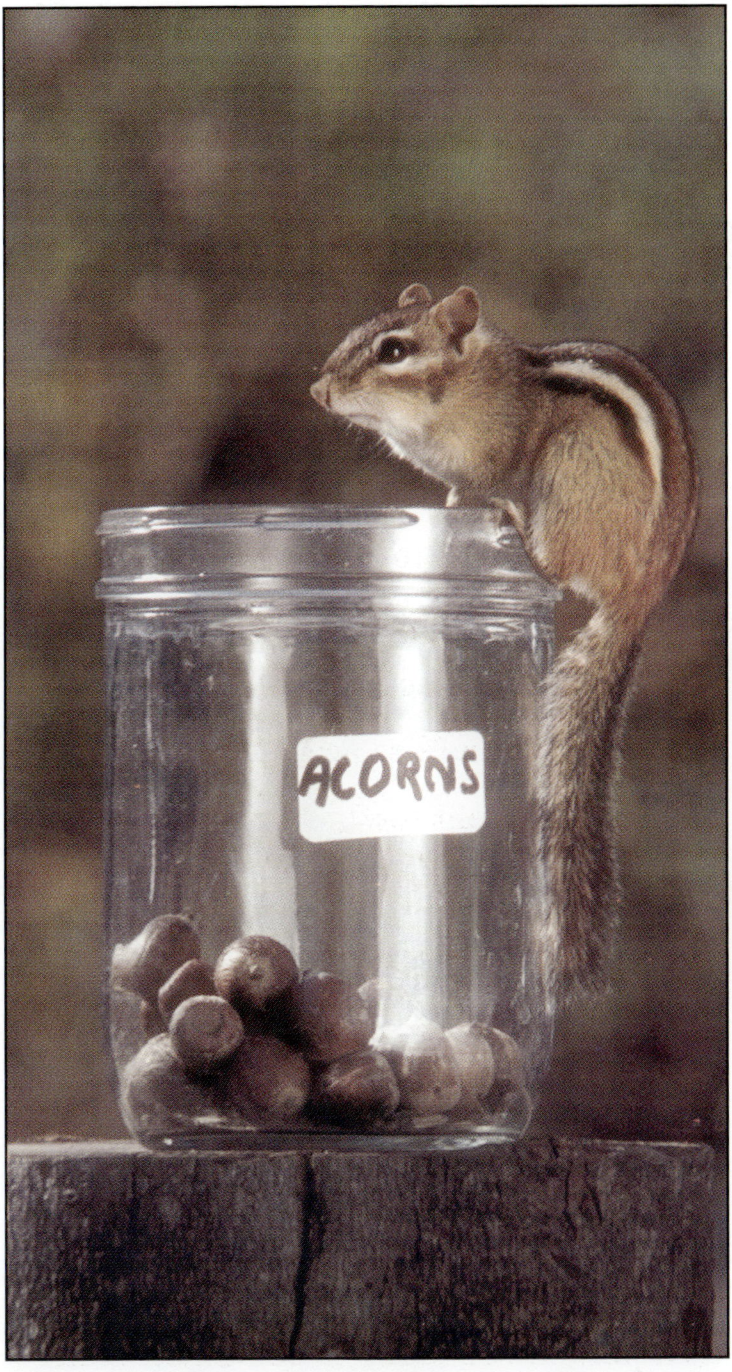
ACORNS

CHIPMUNKS

acorns! But chipmunks love many other kinds of seeds, too. Chippie can carry about thirty kernels of corn in his pouches or about sixty sunflower seeds. But even nine acorns, thirty kernels of corn, and sixty sunflower seeds would not begin to cover the bottom of a bushel basket. You can imagine the hundreds of trips a chipmunk must make to get ready for winter. Wouldn't you call him a hard worker?

🐾 Do You Remember?

Write the correct answer in the blank.

1. A burrow is a chipmunk's ___*home*___.

2. A chipmunk will store only ___*nuts and seeds*___ and ___*seeds*___ in his house.

3. A chipmunk carries nuts and seeds in a ___*pouch*___ on each side of his mouth.

— CHIPMUNKS

Winter Time

As the days get cooler and cooler, every good chipmunk's pile of nuts and seeds gets higher and higher. When the pile of food is so high that his bed almost touches the ceiling, Chippie's work will be done. It will be time for Chippie to snuggle up on his bed of leaves. The busy little fellow must be very tired by now. He curls up and falls fast asleep on his bed of leaves.

Every few days he will wake up hungry. When he does, he will reach under his bed for a snack and then go back to sleep. On sunny winter days he may leave his burrow for a drink, but most of the winter Chippie will stay on his leaf bed atop the nuts and seeds.

What a happy day it is when Chippie can come out of his burrow in spring! Chipmunks are very friendly. They will run to each other's burrows as if to say, "Hello!

CHIPMUNKS

Did you have a nice nap?" Then they will sit and "talk" and "sing" to each other.

Would you like to make friends with a chipmunk? You must remember that they are very shy animals. They scare very easily and run away. But if you stand very still and leave nuts, seeds, and small pieces of bread on the ground for them day after day, a chipmunk might one day hop right up to you as if to say, "Well, what do you have for me today?"

The Bible says

"He that gathereth in summer is a wise son: but he that sleepeth in harvest is a son that causeth shame." —Proverbs 10:5

🐾 Do You Remember?

Circle the correct answer.

1. A chipmunk stays in his burrow in winter.

   (Yes)   No

2. What does the chipmunk do with the food he stores?

   (a) eats it on rainy days

   (b) shares it with other animals

   ((c)) eats it during the winter

3. Chipmunks are very shy. They are easily _____.

   (a) captured

   ((b)) scared

   (c) made into pets

👣 What Do You Think?

1. How is the chipmunk a wise creature?
2. What are some wise things boys and girls can do to be ready for the future?

Great American Songbirds

We can be very thankful to our Creator for the chirps and whistles of songbirds that cheer our day. The three different songbirds that you will read about are probably the most popular songbirds in the United States. Every boy and girl should recognize the colorful robin and the bright red cardinal. And, although the song sparrow is not so colorful, you will find that it has a beauty that is all its own.

There are hundreds of different kinds of songbirds. Although each kind is different, there are some facts that are true about every songbird.

First of all, nearly every bird has its own territory. This means that there are certain trees, bushes, and land that the bird considers his own private property. He will do his best to chase away any other bird that enters his territory. Most birds seem to respect the rights of other birds. A bird will not usually fly into the territory of another bird unless he wants a good fight.

Next, all songbirds are perching birds. Any bird that you see sitting on a telephone wire or that can cling to a twig of a tree is a perching bird. A perching bird has three toes pointed forward and one pointed backward. Because of this, perching birds can grasp a thin twig or a telephone wire.

Have you ever wondered how a sleeping bird perched on a twig or a wire keeps from falling off? When a sleepy bird perches for a nap, it bends its legs. This tightens a tough, cordlike tissue called a tendon, which is in the bird's foot. As long as the bird sleeps, its legs are bent. As long as its legs are bent, the feet cannot let go of the twig or telephone wire. It is not until the bird stands up or straightens out its legs that the tendon loosens and the foot can let go of the twig or wire.

The study of birds is very interesting. How many birds can you name? Can you name any perching birds? Maybe you can think of a bird that you would like to study. As you learn more about birds, you will appreciate more and more the wisdom of our Creator.

🐾 Do You Remember?

Fill in each blank with the correct word.

(a) perching   (b) tendon   (c) territory

1. The trees, bushes, and land that a bird stays in are called his ___territory___.

2. A bird with three toes pointed forward and one backward is a ___perching___ bird.

3. When a perching bird sits on a limb and bends his legs, the ___tendon___ in his foot tightens.

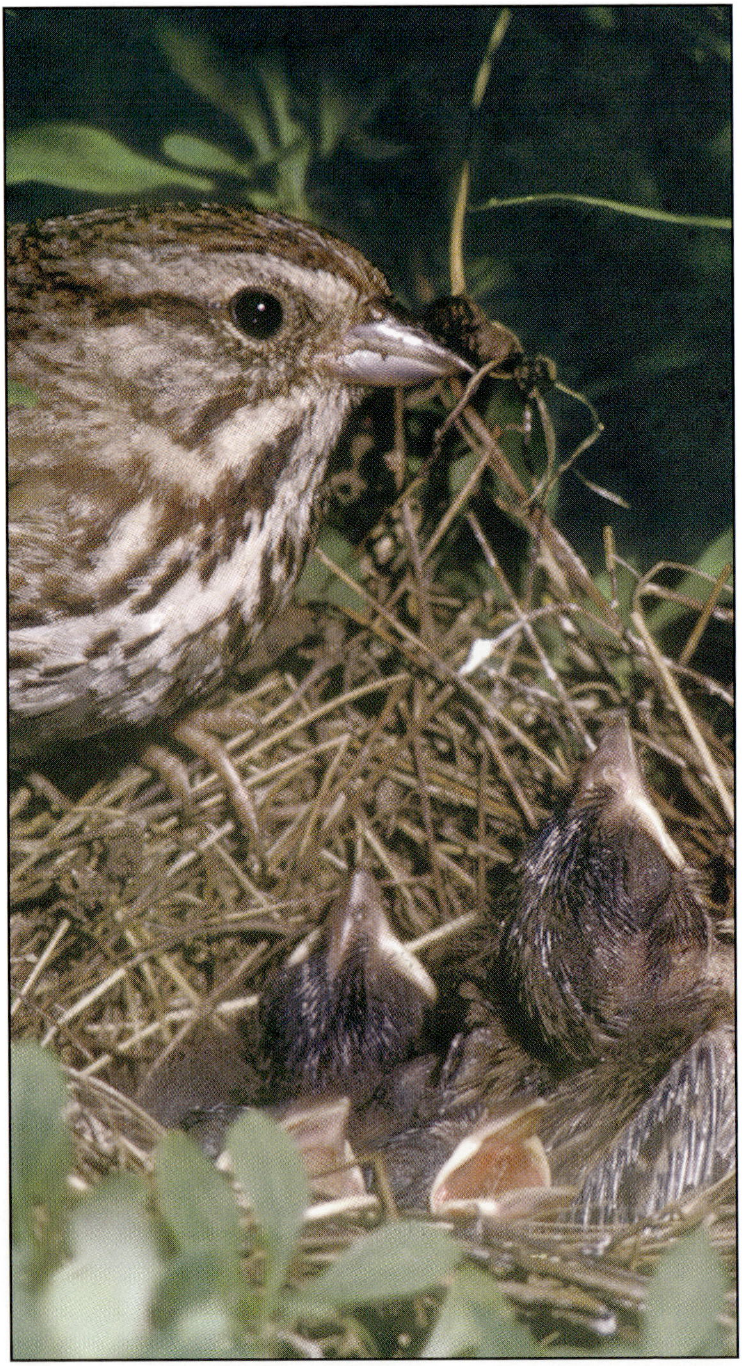

THE SONG SPARROW

Nesting Time

How wonderful the first bird songs of the spring sound to our ears! One of the first birds to sing a cheery welcome to spring is the little song sparrow.

When you speak of these little brown-backed songbirds, do not just say "sparrows," for there are over fifty different kinds of sparrows. You can tell a song sparrow by its white breast marked with black streaks. These streaks run together into one large spot in the center of its breast.

Song sparrows like to build their nests in bushes or low trees. You will rarely ever find a song sparrow's nest in a tall tree. You may find their nests on the ground covered by the low branches of a shrub. Here the nest is protected from the wind and the rain.

The Song Sparrow

As the mother song sparrow works to build the nest, the father bird sings to her. When the nest is finished, it looks like a cup. The outside is made of coarse grass and the stems of plants. The inside of the nest is lined with hair and soft grass.

The mother usually lays three or four white or greenish eggs that are speckled with brown. As she keeps the eggs warm by sitting on them, the father sings to her and brings her food to eat. He also guards the nest.

If an enemy does come near the nest, the father song sparrow will try to lead it away. Sometimes he will pretend to have a broken wing. Fluttering and hobbling, he will lead the enemy away from the nest. Then, just as the enemy is about to catch him, he flies away.

The Song Sparrow

Other birds may fly into the song sparrow's territory and may even try to bother the song sparrow's nest. The song sparrow feels just like you would feel if a robber entered your home. The father sparrow will fight by beating its wings against the other bird and pecking it with his bill until he chases the enemy away.

🐾 Do You Remember?

Circle the correct answer.

1. Song sparrows build their nests _____.

    (a) in tall trees

    (b) by a stream

    (c) on the ground covered with branches of a shrub

2. The father sparrow may pretend he has a broken wing _____.

    (a) to get the attention of the mother sparrow

    (b) to fool the enemy and keep him from the babies

    (c) to trick other creatures to come close enough for him to catch them

3. While the mother sparrow builds the nest and hatches the eggs, the father sparrow _____ and _____.

    (a) helps her

    (b) sings to her

    (c) catches food

THE SONG SPARROW

Busy Parents

After the eggs hatch, the father and mother constantly fly back and forth with caterpillars, grubs, and insects for their young to eat. The busy little song sparrows do not know it, but they are also helping us get rid of many insect pests from our gardens. This job keeps both the parents busy, for it seems the babies' beaks are always wide open waiting for more food to be dropped into them!

In about three weeks the young song sparrows will begin leaving their nest and finding their own food. When cold weather comes, they will probably fly south for the winter. In the spring, they will return with their cheery notes to gladden and warm our hearts.

🐾 Do You Remember?

How are the mother and father song sparrow helping us as they feed their babies?

_____

_____

_____

_____

The Song Sparrow

📖 The Bible says

"Are not two sparrows sold for a farthing? and one of them shall not fall on the ground without your Father.

But the very hairs of your head are all numbered.

Fear ye not therefore, ye are of more value than many sparrows." —*Matthew 10:29–31*

Think of This!

A farthing is not worth more than a couple of pennies—that's all two sparrows are worth, and yet not one of them can be hurt without God the Father knowing about it. The Bible tells us that we are worth much more than sparrows. If God cares this much for each little sparrow, think of how much more He cares for you!

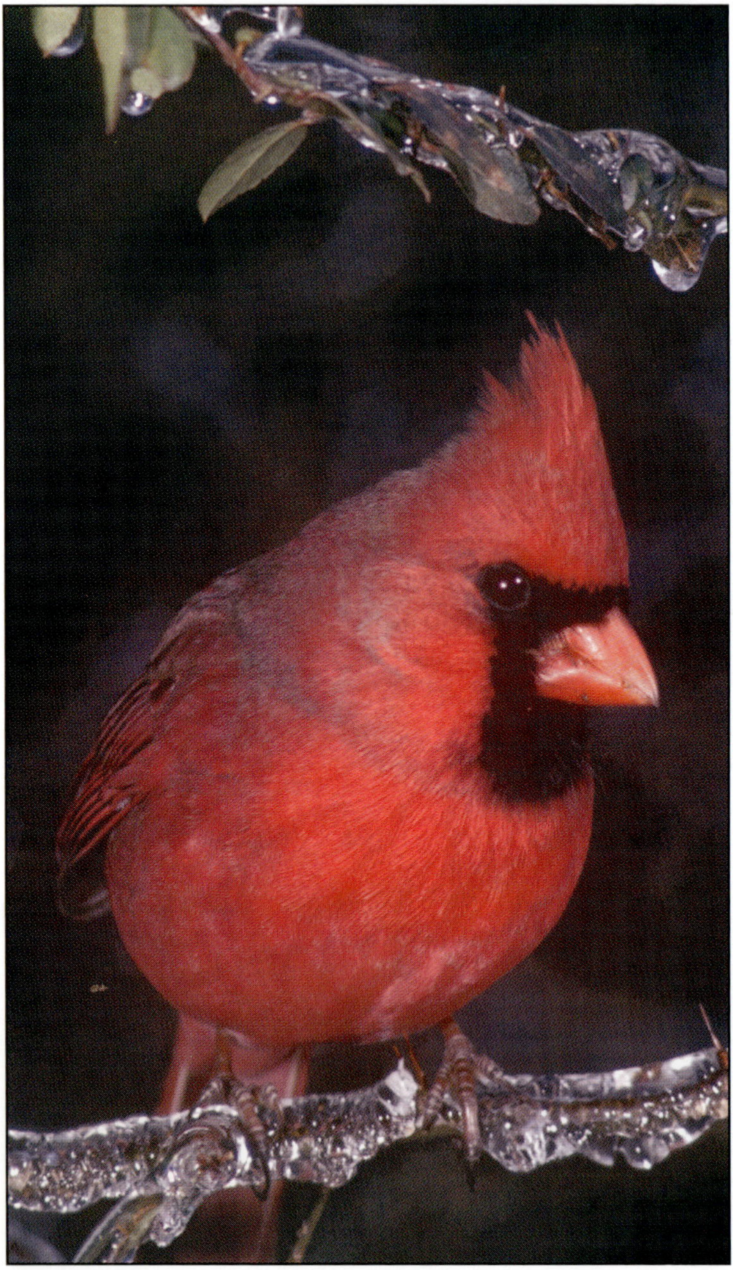

CARDINALS

What Cardinals Are Like

Many birds may look alike to you. Sometimes it is hard to tell one kind of bird from another. The cardinal is one bird, however, that is never difficult to recognize, for there is no other bird colored like the cardinal.

The father cardinal has a bright red coat of feathers with a red crest or peak on top of his head. He looks like he has a black mask over most of his face. The mother bird is not dressed as brightly. Her feathers are brownish with only a touch of red on her crest, wings, and tail feathers.

You may know cardinals by their nickname, "redbird." "Cheer-cheer-cheer!" they seem to call in merry whistling notes.

CARDINALS

Once cardinals move into an area, they will seldom ever leave. They will stay in that area all year long. Even in the North, they stay through the cold, snowy winter. Can you imagine what a beautiful sight it is to see a bright red cardinal against the white snow?

Because cardinals do not mind the hardships of winter, you may have already guessed that they are very brave birds. Father cardinals will fight any bird that dares come into their territory, even another cardinal. Then how the feathers fly!

🐾 Do You Remember?

Circle the correct answer.

1. The father cardinal is more brightly colored than the mother.

    (Yes)   No

2. The crest is found on the cardinal's _____.

    (a) head   (b) wing

3. When the weather gets cold, cardinals will _____.

    (a) fly south for the winter
    (b) stay in their same territory

CARDINALS

Building a Nest

When nesting time comes in the spring, the mother bird flies around to find a good, safe place for her nest. She carefully looks over many bushes, shrubs, and small trees before she chooses a place. Then she begins building. The father will hardly ever help, but he will keep her company and sing her pretty songs.

It may take as long as five days for the mother cardinal to build her nest. She makes it out of twigs, stems, dried leaves, and pieces of bark. To finish the nest, she lines the inside with soft, dried grass.

After waiting a few days, the mother cardinal begins to lay eggs. She will lay one egg each day until she has three or four

CARDINALS

eggs in her nest. Only after she has finished laying eggs will she begin to sit on them.

While she is sitting on the eggs, the father will fly back and forth bringing seeds, berries, and insects for her to eat. When she does leave the nest to get a drink, the father carefully guards the nest. There are many animals that like to eat bird eggs.

In only twelve days the baby redbirds begin to chip their way through the shells. When they first hatch, cardinals have no feathers at all and their eyes are tightly closed. But by the time they are ten days old, their bodies are covered with soft brown feathers. And they are always begging for something to eat!

Do You Remember?
Write the correct answer in the blank.

1. The time for building nests and starting families is called _____.

2. While the mother cardinal builds the nest, the father will _____ to her.

3. While the mother cardinal is hatching the eggs, the father brings her _____.

CARDINALS

Word Practice

1. Write the root word.

    (a) apart _____part_____

    (b) beautiful _____beauty_____

    (c) whistling _____whistle_____

    (d) dried _____dry_____

2. Find three compound words in this story. Write them.

    (a) _____meanwhile_____

    (b) _____something_____

    (c) _____redbird_____

The Young Leave Their Nest

Before long the young cardinals try to fly and leave the nest. This is a very dangerous time for the young redbirds. Their wings are not yet strong enough to fly far or fast. So when they first leave their nest, the father takes over caring for them. He makes sure they find enough food. He also watches out for the cat, the skunk, the raccoon, and other animals who like to eat young birds.

Meanwhile the mother cardinal is busy, too. She is building another nest. Cardinal parents raise two or three families in the spring and early summer.

By the end of the summer, each of the young redbirds will have lost its brown "baby feathers." The hard-working parents

CARDINALS

are very busy finding enough insects to feed themselves and all their hungry youngsters.

Did you ever stop to think that the cardinal parents are doing us a favor? Think of how many more caterpillars, potato bugs, and other insect pests there would be in our gardens destroying our food if it were not for all the bold cardinal families catching insects to feed their young! "Cheer-cheer-cheer!"

The Bible says

"He hath made everything beautiful in His time." —*Ecclesiastes 3:11*

🐾 Do You Remember?

Write the correct answer in the blank.

1. While the father trains and cares for the young cardinals, the mother _builds a nest_.

2. The time of learning to fly is dangerous for young cardinals because _animals can catch them_.

3. How do cardinals help people with gardens?
   cardinals eat the bugs

🐾 What Do You Think?

1. What different jobs do the mother and father cardinal each have to do?

2. Do all of God's people have the same things to do for Him? Why?

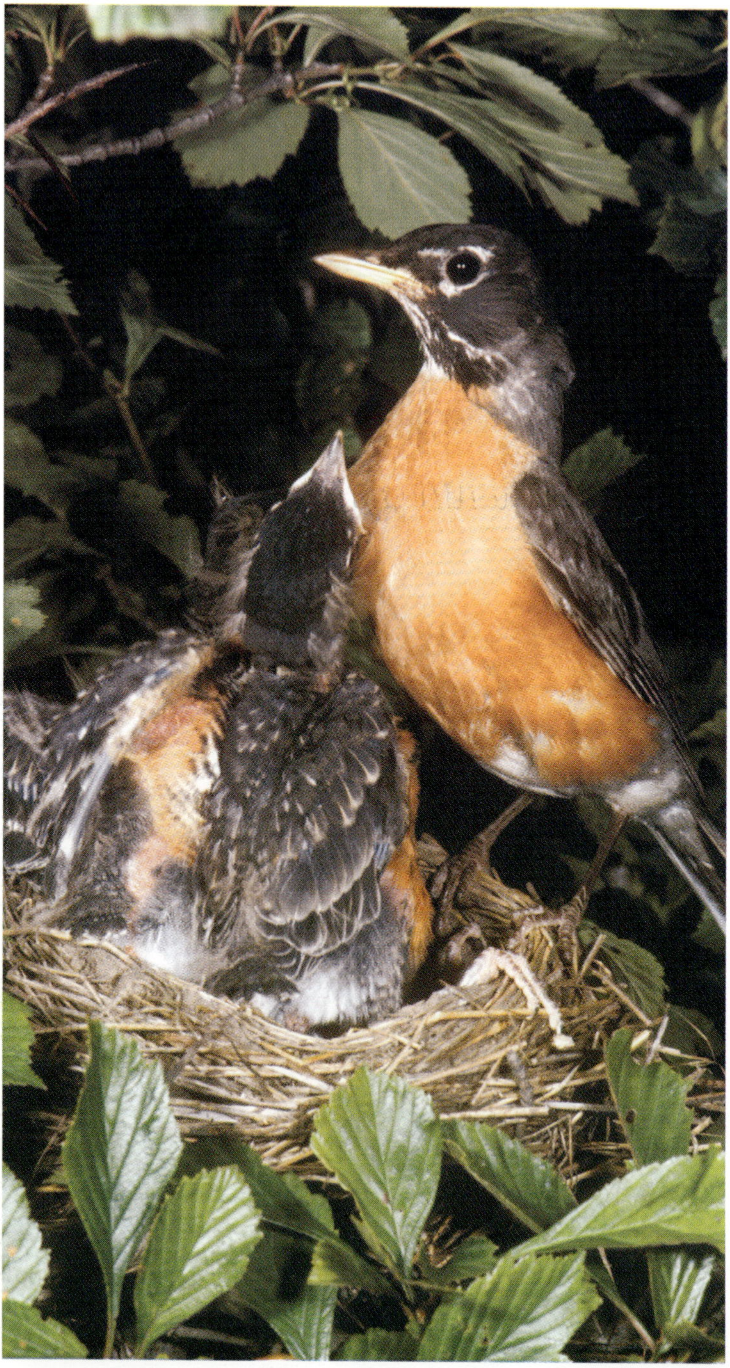

ROBINS

Meet the Robins

When English people first came to live in America, they saw a bird that reminded them of the red-breasted robin that lives in England. They called it a robin, too. That red-breasted bird they saw, however, really belongs to the thrush family of birds. But even today we still call this bird by the name the English people gave it by mistake—the robin.

ROBINS

The cold winter winds still blow during the last week of February and the first weeks of March. There may still be a blanket of snow on the ground in the North. Yet one bird has already returned from its winter stay in the sunny South—Mr. Robin! Although the snow makes food hard to find, he puffs out his red breast and sings, "Cheer up! Cheer up!" When we hear the robin's song, we know warm spring days are not far away.

A few weeks afterward, when the snow melts, Mrs. Robin flies north to join her mate. The trees have begun to bud. The ground is not frozen anymore. The earthworms have begun crawling. This is just what the robins have been waiting for.

The robins hop quickly across the ground, stop, and cock their heads. When one spies an earthworm, it will grab hold with its beak and pull and pull and pull. It looks like a game of tug-of-war, doesn't it? The robin doesn't always win, but usually the earthworm tires out and lets go. Then it becomes the robin's dinner.

Robins

🐾 Do You Remember?

Circle the correct answer.

1. A mate is a _____.

    (a) friend   (b) partner   (c) child

2. When a robin tries to pull a worm from the ground, _____ usually wins.

    (a) the robin

    (b) the worm

    (c) the babies

3. Robins spend most of the winter in a cold place.

    Yes   No

Building Their Nest

Now it's time for the robins to begin building their nest. Together they search for a safe place. Robins seem to like being around people. Often they will build their nest in a tree near a house, under the edge of the roof, or even on a porch.

The robins gather pieces of grass, string, paper, twigs, and other bits of things which they make into a cup-shaped nest. After the nest is formed, they begin to plaster the sides of it with mud. Back and forth they fly from water puddles, scooping up mud with their beaks and carrying it to the nest. This takes many trips. Their beaks are very small. No wonder they stop to rest and eat a few earthworms.

But then it's back to work. Mrs. Robin hops into the newly mud-plastered nest.

Robins

She works the soft mud into the grass with her beak. Then with her breast she pushes against the moist walls, shaping the nest to fit her. The next step is the easiest—letting the mud dry. A whole week has passed since Mr. and Mrs. Robin began working.

If the robins left the nest this way, however, it would be very hard and uncomfortable. So when the nest is dry, Mrs. Robin lines it with grass.

Now she is ready to lay her eggs. What a beautiful blue her first egg is! In the next three days she will lay three more blue eggs. Mr. Robin stays close by, singing to his mate and guarding his territory.

🐾 Do You Remember?
Write the correct answer in the blank.

1. Robins seem to like to be near *people*.

2. The inside of the robin's nest is plastered with *mud*.

3. Robins often build nests near *house ground*.

ROBINS

God's Protection Plan

You have probably noticed that Mr. and Mrs. Robin do not look alike. Mr. Robin has a bright red breast. Mrs. Robin's is a dull brownish-red. The rest of her body is a lighter color, too. This is God's way of protecting her and her nest. The mother robin's lighter colors help to make her look like the color of the nest. The dull colors make it hard for other animals to see her and the nest. If she were brightly colored, both she and her nest would be easily spotted.

The brightly colored father does not sit on the nest. If an enemy does come near the nest, the brave father tries his best to lead it away. Seeing his bright colors, the enemy quickly forgets about the dull-colored nest and follows after him. After Mr. Robin leads the enemy away, he quickly flies to safety.

You will find that most mother birds are not as brightly colored as the fathers. You may even hear some people call the mother birds ugly. But if you stop and think about it, a mother bird's dull colors are a very beautiful part of God's creation and protection.

The spring brings rain. If the eggs get wet, they will not hatch. Mrs. Robin seems to know this. She spreads her wings wide over the nest. The rain runs off her feathers, and the eggs stay dry.

Robins

It may rain for many days. If it does, Mrs. Robin stays right with the nest, keeping the eggs dry. During a long rain, the father tries to find food for his mate. He seems to know that she cannot leave the nest. You think you are glad to see the sun after a rainy day. Think how happy the robins must be!

🐾 Do You Remember?

Circle the correct answer.

1. Circle the things that are true about the mother robin.

    (a) bright red breast

    (b) lighter colored body

    (c) dull brownish-red breast

    (d) sings

2. While the mother robin hatches the eggs, the father's two jobs are to _try to feed mother_ and _keep enmy away_

    (a) find food

    (b) keep rain off the nest

    (c) guard the nest

3. Mrs. Robin keeps her eggs dry by _____.

    (a) making the nest with a cover on it

    (b) spreading her wings over the nest in the rain

    (c) building the nest in a dry place

ROBINS

A New Family to Care For

Thirteen days have passed since Mrs. Robin laid her last egg. The egg shells begin to crack as the baby robins peck their way through the shells. They hardly look like birds at all. They have no feathers. Their heads look huge. It will take a few days of growing before these babies even look like birds.

Meanwhile the proud father realizes his children need to eat. Off he flies for the favorite food of baby robins—fat, juicy earthworms! At the end of the day, the tired robin parents tuck their heads under a wing and sleep until the early morning hours. Then the hungry chirps of their young family, calling for more earthworms, wake them up. We can hardly see anything else but their open mouths as they wait for their father or mother to stuff worms down their throats.

The baby robins look greedy, but young robins need all this food because they grow so fast. Growing takes energy. Energy comes from food. In one day, a baby robin eats more than its weight in earthworms.

You could never expect to eat as much food as you weigh, because children do not grow as fast as birds. In only two weeks from the time they hatch, the baby robins will have grown their feathers, then in a few days they will be flying. No human baby

ROBINS

can walk when it is only two weeks old, because human babies grow much more slowly than birds. Perhaps this helps you understand why a baby robin needs so much energy—and so many earthworms!

Just how many earthworms does a baby robin eat? If we could lay earthworms from end to end, a baby robin would eat more than twelve feet of earthworms each day. And that is just one baby robin. There are four in this nest. It's a good thing God placed thousands of earthworms in one acre of soil, isn't it?

When the young robins do leave their nest, the father keeps his eye on them. He seems to know that their wings are not very strong yet. It would be easy for a cat or some other animal to catch the young robins. But soon they will be able to take care of themselves. And soon Mr. and Mrs. Robin will build a new nest for another family.

🐾 Do You Remember?
Write the correct answer in the blank.

1. A baby robin's favorite food is ___*earthworms*___.

2. When robins are first born, the biggest part of their body is their ___*head*___.

3. Young robins need so much food because they ___*grow*___ so fast.

🐾 What Do You Think?

1. Do the mother and father robin look exactly alike? Why?

2. How has God made you different from other boys and girls? Why?

Animals from Around the World

It is fun to read about animals from all over the world. There are many kinds of animals that cannot live anywhere else but where God placed them, except perhaps in zoos. But the zoos must then care for the animal as if it were back in its own homeland.

Some animals are difficult to find. Most of us can only enjoy them by reading about them. The giant panda from China, the ostrich from Africa, and the sea otters from the cold ocean waters are three such animals. Yet each one lives an interesting life—a life you will enjoy reading about.

There are many different animals in each country of the world. We could travel from country to country this whole world over and still never see all the animals of God's creation. Can you even begin to imagine the greatness and the wisdom of God Who not only created them, but also cares for each one?

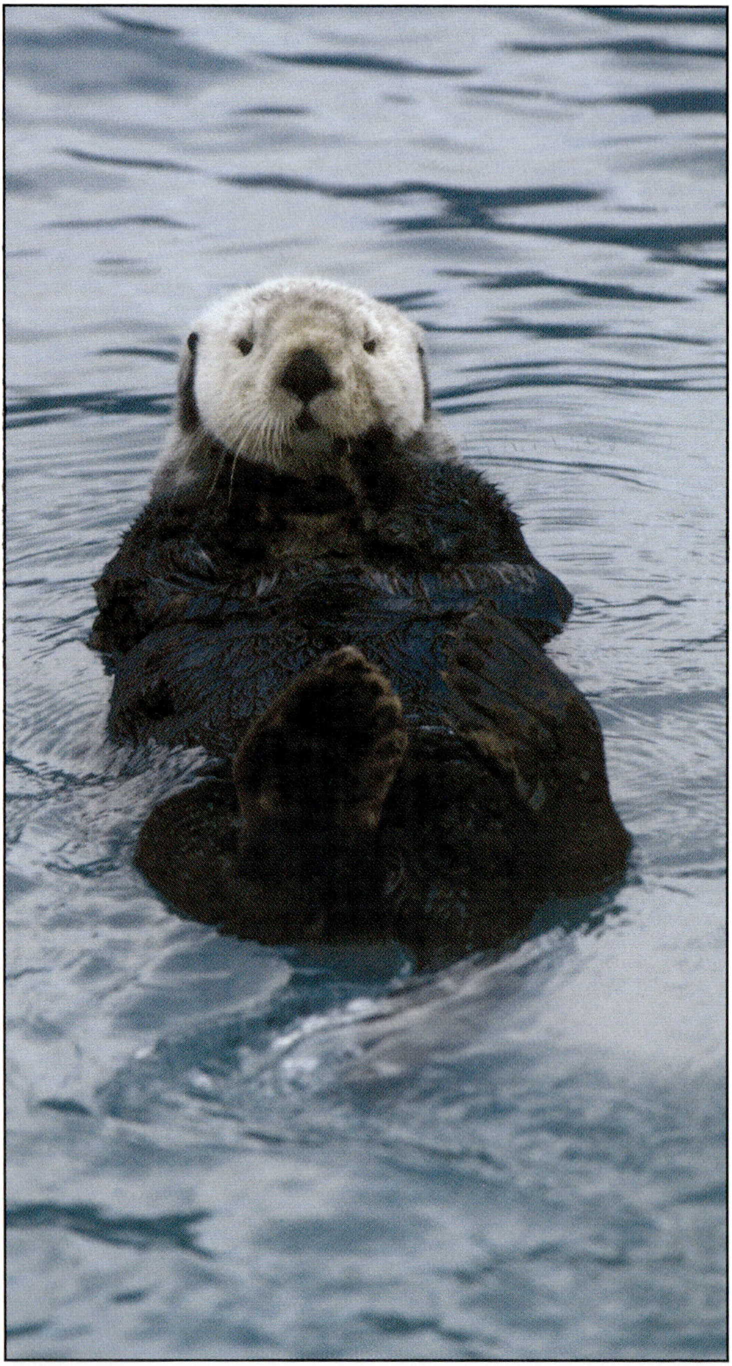

Sea Otters

Meet the Sea Otters

Have you ever been fishing in a boat on a windy day? You probably felt like a cork bobbing up and down with the waves. It may have been fun for a little while, but would you like to bob up and down all day long, every day of the year?

God created one animal that enjoys nothing better than bobbing up and down on its back in the ocean—the sea otter. In fact, a stormy, wave-tossed sea is the otter's delight!

A sea otter has a beautiful dark brown, almost black, fur coat. It has small but

> **Words to watch for**
>
> **kelp**—a seaweed that grows from the floor of the ocean up to the ocean's surface
> **oxygen**—a gas from the air
> **exhale**—to breathe out

Sea Otters

strong front paws which it uses like fingers. Since its hind feet are webbed and its tail is flat, the otter is an excellent swimmer. Sea otters can weigh up to eighty pounds and can grow to be four feet long. They are the biggest of all the kinds of otters.

Sea otters usually stay in groups near an island of kelp, a floating raft of seaweed. Here you will see mother otters floating on their backs, holding their babies, or cubs, on their chests.

🐾 Do You Remember?

Circle the correct answer.

1. Baby sea otters are called _____.

    (a) kids (b) cubs (c) kits

2. Circle those things that help the otter to swim.

    (a) flat tail

    (b) webbed feet

    (c) paws like fingers

3. Kelp is _____.

    (a) a plant (b) an animal (c) a boat

Barney

One little cub has just been born. We'll call him Barney. The mother combs Barney's hair with her claws and brushes his fur with her paws until the cub's fur is soft and fluffy. How the mother loves her baby. She would give her life to protect him.

Sea Otters

Barney enjoys the free ride his mother gives him. Soon he is fast asleep. The hungry mother slides him off her chest and lays him in the water where he will float until his mother returns.

To keep Barney from floating away, the mother otter wraps a piece of kelp around him. The kelp acts like a giant leash chained to the ocean's floor. It will hold Barney in one place. The gentle waves rock him as if he were in a cradle.

🐾 Do You Remember?

Write the correct answer in the blank.

1. A baby sea otter rides on his mother's _____chest_____.

2. How does Barney get his hair combed and fur brushed? __his mothers claws and paws.__

3. Barney's mother wraps him with a piece of ____kelp____ to keep him from floating away as he sleeps.

Getting a Bite to Eat

On her way to find food, mother otter lets out her breath and dives deep into the ocean. If she did not let out her breath, she would not stay under the water long. Her lungs act like balloons. When a balloon is full of air, will it stay under the water by

Sea Otters

itself? Of course not. It bobs right back up. And so the sea otter would bob right back up if she forgot to let her breath out.

How long can a sea otter hold its breath? For as long as five minutes! You can't do that, but then you do not need to find your dinner under the water! God created the sea otter in a wonderful way. While the otter rests on top of the water, it is storing oxygen in its blood. When the otter dives, it uses the stored oxygen. The sea otter must come to the ocean's surface to breathe when the oxygen gets low.

Otters eat crabs, snails, clams, and small fish, but their favorite food is sea urchins. It is a good thing, too. Many small ocean animals live in the leaves and stems of kelp, including the sea urchins. But the sea urchins eat the stems of the kelp. Then the kelp floats away and dies. Dead kelp can no longer be a home for any animal. Can you see God's plan in giving the sea otter a special taste for sea urchins?

Today mother sea otter is lucky. She finds a clam, a sea urchin, and a smooth stone. Tucking the clam and the stone under her arm, she holds the sea urchin in her front paws and swims to the surface.

Sea Otters

First she checks on Barney, who is still fast asleep. Then she rolls over on her back. Her chest becomes a table where she lays the clam and sea urchin. By now you must be wondering why she brought the stone. With the stone she pounds against the shells of the clam and the sea urchin until she breaks them apart. Then she has a feast.

When she finishes, there are bits of shells and scraps of food left on her "table." To clean her table, she rolls over and over in the water.

Barney is awake and hungry by now. He cries like a baby would for his mother. Mother otter puts Barney back on her chest. Bobbing up and down on his mother, he now has his dinner of warm milk from her.

Sea Otters

🐾 Do You Remember?
Circle the correct answer.

1. An otter lets the air out of its lungs so it can _____.

    (a) float better

    (b) stay under water longer ⟵ *circled*

    (c) have a table on its chest

2. It is important that otters like to eat sea urchins because the sea urchins _____.

    (a) destroy the kelp where otters and other sea animals live ⟵ *circled*

    (b) eat kelp seeds so no more can grow

    (c) attack baby otters

3. Otters like to eat _____.

    (a) kelp

    (b) crabs and snails ⟵ *circled*

    (c) shells and stones ⟵ *circled*

Swimming Lessons for Barney

When will Barney start swimming? As soon as a sea otter is born it can float, but it cannot swim. All sea otter cubs have to have swimming lessons!

During the first lesson, mother otter turns Barney face down in the water. Did you like getting your face wet the first time? No! Neither does Barney. Getting his face wet scares him. Barney cries and screams until he gets used to getting his face wet. Hearing his cries may bother his mother, but she knows her cub has to learn to swim, and so she keeps making him get his face wet.

At last he doesn't mind the water splashing against his face. But now he must learn to kick his hind feet. They are webbed like a duck's to help him swim

Sea Otters

better. Weeks go by until the cub finally learns how to swim.

After Barney learns to swim, he must begin his diving lessons. It takes much longer to learn how to dive. Until Barney learns to exhale, or let the air out of his lungs, he will bob right back up on top of the water. How patient his mother is as she keeps showing him, but Barney does not seem to understand.

Swimming over to Barney, the mother breathes out her air into his ear and then dives. Barney waits for his mother to come back up.

One day, Barney finally understands what he is to do. Playfully he swims over to her. First he breathes in. Then he breathes out all his air and dives! How proud Barney's mother is of her cub, and how proud Barney is of himself! What a great sport diving is now!

The loving mother will play all kinds of games with her cub to teach him to swim better and faster. In fact, all of the otters like to join in, because otters are very playful animals.

Sea Otters

Young otters toss and catch balls of kelp. They may chase each other in a game of tag. With a long broken stem of kelp, they play a game of tug of war. And the whole family, old and young, joins in a game of hide-and-seek! Are you surprised? Did you think boys and girls were the only ones who knew about these games?

At night each sea otter rolls over on its back in the chilly ocean water. Mothers with cubs take their young up in their arms and put them on their chests where they sleep all night. To keep from floating away, each sea otter wraps a piece of kelp around its body. All night long, rocked by the ocean waves, the otters enjoy their sleep.

SEA OTTERS

Do You Remember?
Write the correct answer in the blank.

1. When you exhale, you breathe ~~all~~ out.

2. What does a baby sea otter learn during its first swimming lesson?

   to put his head under

3. At night sea otters sleep with a piece of kelp wrapped around them. Why?

   so they don't float away

Word Practice
Write the root word.

created — create
bobbing — bob
diving — dive
fishing — fish
tossed — toss

chilly _chill_
windy _wind_
swimmer _swim_

What Do You Think?

1. How did God design the sea otter to live in the sea? What special abilities did He give it?

2. What is special about us? How did God create us different from any other creatures?

3. What games do sea otters play that remind you of children's games?

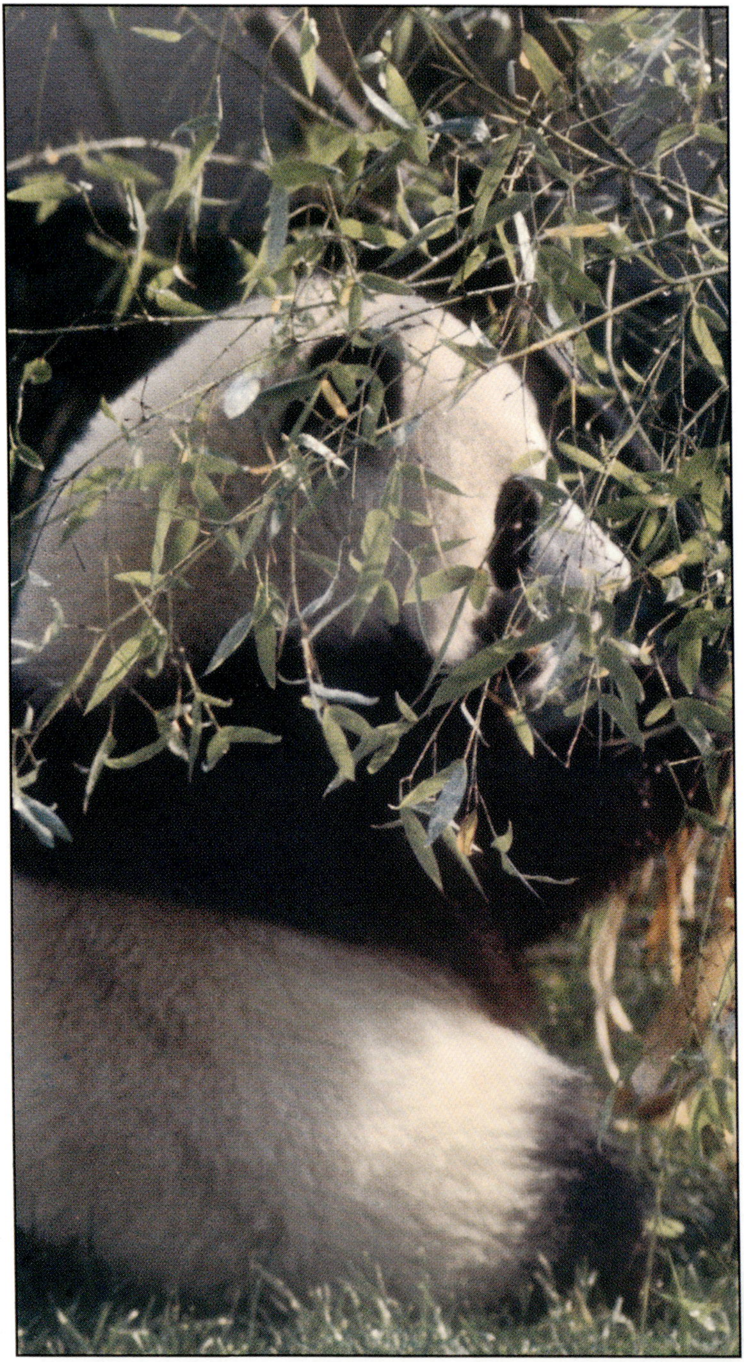

THE GIANT PANDA

The Panda's Jungle

The jungles in western China are quite different from other jungles you may have read about. In the jungles of western China there are mountains 5,000 to 14,000 feet high. Instead of the trees and vines found in most jungles, bamboo grows so thick it is impossible to see very far ahead. And instead of the hot, humid days you think of in tropical jungles, you may see snow, especially high in the mountains.

Bamboo is a woody grass. In China, bamboo stalks grow from ten to fifteen feet tall. That is twice as tall as a man. In the spring

---

Words to watch for

panda—a large black and white animal that looks much like a bear
bamboo—a tall, woody grass

The Giant Panda

the bamboo is tender, but in the winter the stalks turn tough and dry.

What animals could live in such a jungle? Both brown and black bears live here. So do leopards and wild goats. These animals also live in other parts of the world. But there is one kind of animal that lives only in a bamboo jungle—a panda.

🐾 Do You Remember?

Circle the correct answer.

1. What would you find in a jungle in western China?

   (mountains)   vines   (brown bears)
   (bamboo)   (snow)   (wild goats)
   ostrich   trees   giraffes

2. Bamboo is _____.

   (a) a plant

   (b) an animal

3. The panda lives_____.

   (a) at the North pole

   (b) in a bamboo jungle

   (c) in a tropical jungle

The Giant Panda

A Real, Live Panda

Most people have never seen a real, live panda. Only a few zoos in the United States have pandas. One is the National Zoological Park in Washington, D.C. Why aren't there more pandas in zoos across the country? In the bamboo jungles of China, pandas are hard to find. Even the Chinese people who live near the jungle rarely ever see a panda.

As you have already learned, bamboo grows very thick and very tall. The panda has to make a tunnel or pathway through the bamboo to get around. It is very difficult for a man to walk even a few steps into this jungle without getting lost. And so, it is very difficult to capture a panda for zoos. Besides this, a panda is a very rare animal.

This means that there are not many left, even in their home jungles.

What does a panda look like? If you saw one, you would say it looks like a real, live black and white teddy bear. Its ears look like balls of black fluff on a white head. Its eyes have black circles around them. Its body is white with a black band of fur across the shoulders. All four legs are black, and it has a short, black tail. You may think that a panda's fur looks soft and fluffy, but it is really coarse and wiry.

The Giant Panda

👣 Do You Remember?
Write the correct answer in the blank.

1. Why aren't there many pandas in zoos?

   _____

   _____

   _____

2. A *rare* animal is one that is _____ to find because there aren't very many left.

3. Pandas look most like a real live

   _____.

A Panda's Life

A mother panda with her cub is a very wonderful sight to see. Sitting on her haunches, the proud mother holds her cub in her arms and cuddles it.

It is amazing to know how much growing a panda does. At birth, it weighs less than one pound. By the time it is six months old, it may weigh twenty-five pounds. When full grown, it will weigh from 250 to 300 pounds and will measure about five feet long from nose to tail. A baby panda certainly has a lot of growing to do, doesn't it?

The Giant Panda

What do pandas eat? Think for a moment and take a guess. Pandas live only in bamboo jungles. Their favorite food is bamboo. In fact, they eat about twenty pounds of bamboo each day in their jungle home. In the Washington Zoo, pandas eat bamboo that is grown especially for them right at the zoo.

You would enjoy watching a panda eat. It does not put its head down to the food as most other animals do. While sitting on its haunches, the panda uses its front paws to bring the food up to its mouth. The panda has six claws on its front paws. The sixth claw is used to grasp food and bring it to the panda's mouth.

The Giant Panda

If you ever have a chance to visit the National Zoological Park, you will find the two pandas in separate cages, side by side, in an air-conditioned house. The zoo keepers know that the pandas would rather be alone most of the time. The best time to visit the panda house is at their feeding times. Otherwise you might only see sleeping pandas, because pandas take many naps.

Do You Remember?
Write the correct answer in the blank.

1. Panda babies are called ___cub___.

2. Pandas eat about twenty pounds of ___bamboo___ each day.

3. In the zoo, pandas are kept in separate cages because ___they would rather be alone___.

What Do You Think?

1. Do zookeepers treat all animals exactly alike? Why? What special things does the zookeeper do for a panda?

2. Does God treat all His children alike? Why?

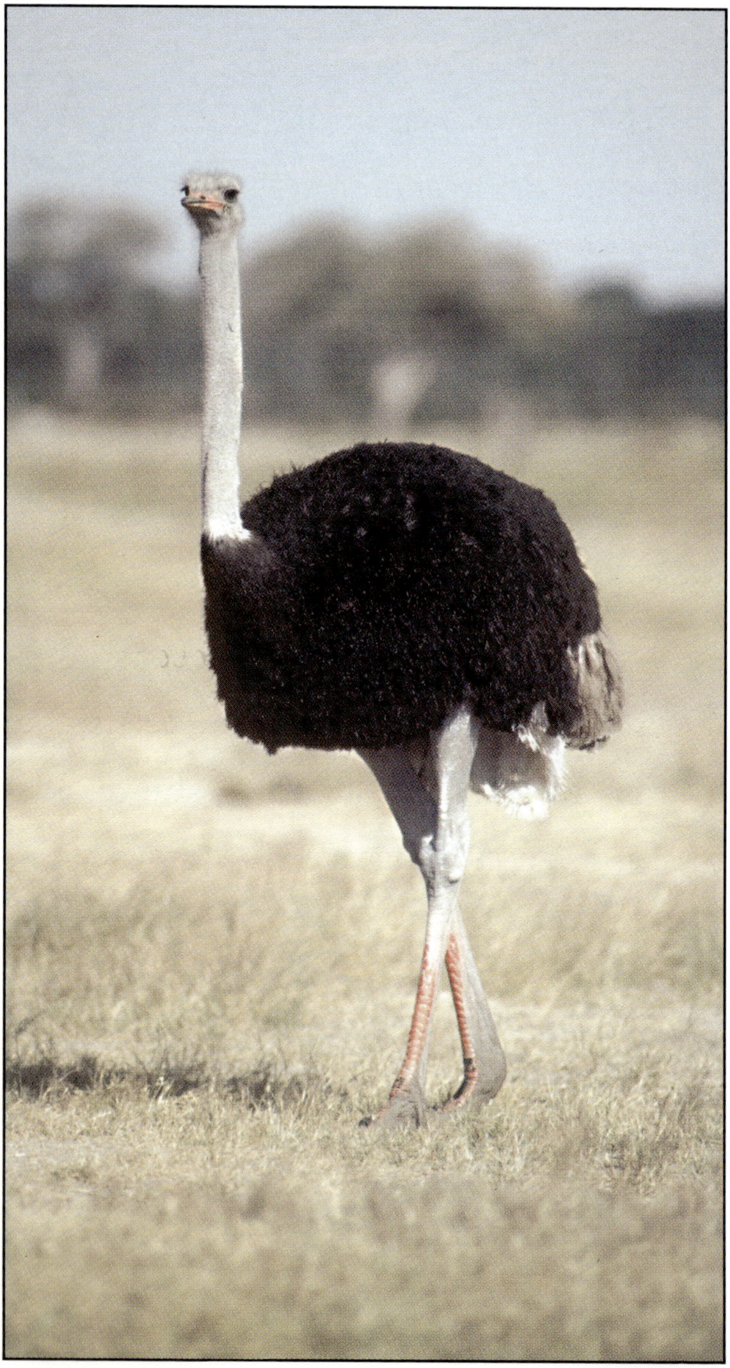

THE LARGEST BIRD

The largest birds in all the world are ostriches. Ostriches live on the plains of Africa and the desert of Arabia. A full-grown ostrich stands anywhere from six to eight feet tall and can weigh up to three hundred or more pounds. Their long legs end in two thick toes—one toe is large and the other is much smaller.

The ostrich's legs may look silly to you, but they are very useful to the ostrich. His long legs and long neck help the ostrich get a better look at things in the distance. If the ostrich sees danger, he has time to

> **Words to watch for**
>
> **height** (hīt)—how tall something is
> **pores**—very, very small holes
> **plain**—a large, flat area of land
> **desert**—dry, sandy land where few plants grow

173

THE LARGEST BIRD

escape. An ostrich's long legs also help the bird run thirty to thirty-five miles per hour! Although the ostrich is a bird, it cannot fly. Some people think his wings help the ostrich keep his balance when he runs so fast.

An ostrich would rather run from danger, but it will fight if danger is too close to run from. His two toenails are very hard and sharp. The ostrich uses them like knives to slash into an animal as well as to give hard, sharp kicks. The ostrich can kill its enemies by fighting with its feet!

The lion is one animal that considers the ostrich to be a very tasty meal. But even the lion usually cannot kill an ostrich unless he sneaks up on an ostrich who does not know he is there.

Do You Remember?

Write the correct answer in the blank.

1. A very flat area of land is a _____plain_____.

2. When danger is close, an ostrich may fight with his _____feet_____.

— THE LARGEST BIRD —

Nesting Time

When it is time for ostriches to start their family, the father and mother dig a large hole in the sand. This hole is the nest in which the mother lays about eight eggs.

Ostrich eggs are hard and shiny. They are creamy white in color and speckled with tiny pores. Each egg is about six to eight inches long and weighs two to three pounds. It would take two dozen (or twenty-four) chicken eggs to equal the size of one ostrich egg. The largest bird in the world also lays the largest egg in the world.

During the night the father sits on the nest. Since his feathers are black and shiny, he is not easily seen, even on a moonlit night. The mother has duller-colored gray feathers. Her duller color helps her to blend

THE LARGEST BIRD

in with the sand, and so she is not easily seen during the day. As the mother sits on the nest, the father ostrich is usually standing guard nearby.

Sometimes the days are so warm that the mother can leave the nest and let the sun warm the eggs. However, at noontime the sun is too hot and would cook the eggs if they were left by themselves. Then the father ostrich comes and stands over the nest, shading the eggs from the hot sun.

Perhaps you have heard that an ostrich buries its head in the sand when danger is near. That is not true. During the day, the mother sits on her nest. If she sees danger coming, she will not leave her nest. She stretches her tall neck along the ground and flattens herself out so she cannot easily be seen. Instead of being a coward, she is really very brave.

🐾 Do You Remember?

Circle the correct answer.

1. The ostrich makes its nest in _____.

   (a) the sand (b) a tree

   (c) a riverbank

2. At night the father ostrich sits on the nest because his shiny, black feathers blend in with the darkness.

   Yes   No

3. When a mother ostrich is hatching eggs and sees danger coming, she _____.

   (a) buries her head in the sand

   (b) cries out for the father ostrich to fight

   (c) stretches her neck along the ground and flattens herself out

THE LARGEST BIRD

Baby Ostriches

Together the parents work to protect their eggs from animals and snakes that would eat them. After six weeks, the proud parents watch as the chicks begin to break through the hard shells.

After the chicks get their heads out of the tough shell, they are too worn out to go any further. They rest for a while, feeling the sun's warm rays for the very first time. Then it's time to go back to work again, pecking the rest of their way out of the hard eggshell. The parents can only watch, for their beaks are much too large to help.

At first the new chicks may sit under their father's warm feathers while he sits on the ground. But soon both parents will make the chicks walk and run to strengthen their legs. In a few days, the chicks are running everywhere catching insects and eating seeds.

The Largest Bird

The young ostriches even swallow pebbles! No, they don't really *eat* the pebbles. Ostriches have no teeth to grind up food before they swallow. The pebbles in their stomachs grind up the food they eat. An ostrich's menu includes snakes, lizards, frogs, insects, and seeds. Everything is swallowed whole. Gulp!

There are many animals that would like to eat baby ostriches, too. If the parents are careful, they can protect them against the bigger animals that roam on the ground. But what about hawks that swoop swiftly down from the sky and fly away with their dinner?

God has made the feathers of a baby ostrich the same color as the grass and sand it lives on. To a hawk in the sky, a baby ostrich looks just like a small bush. When it sees trouble, the chick will flatten itself

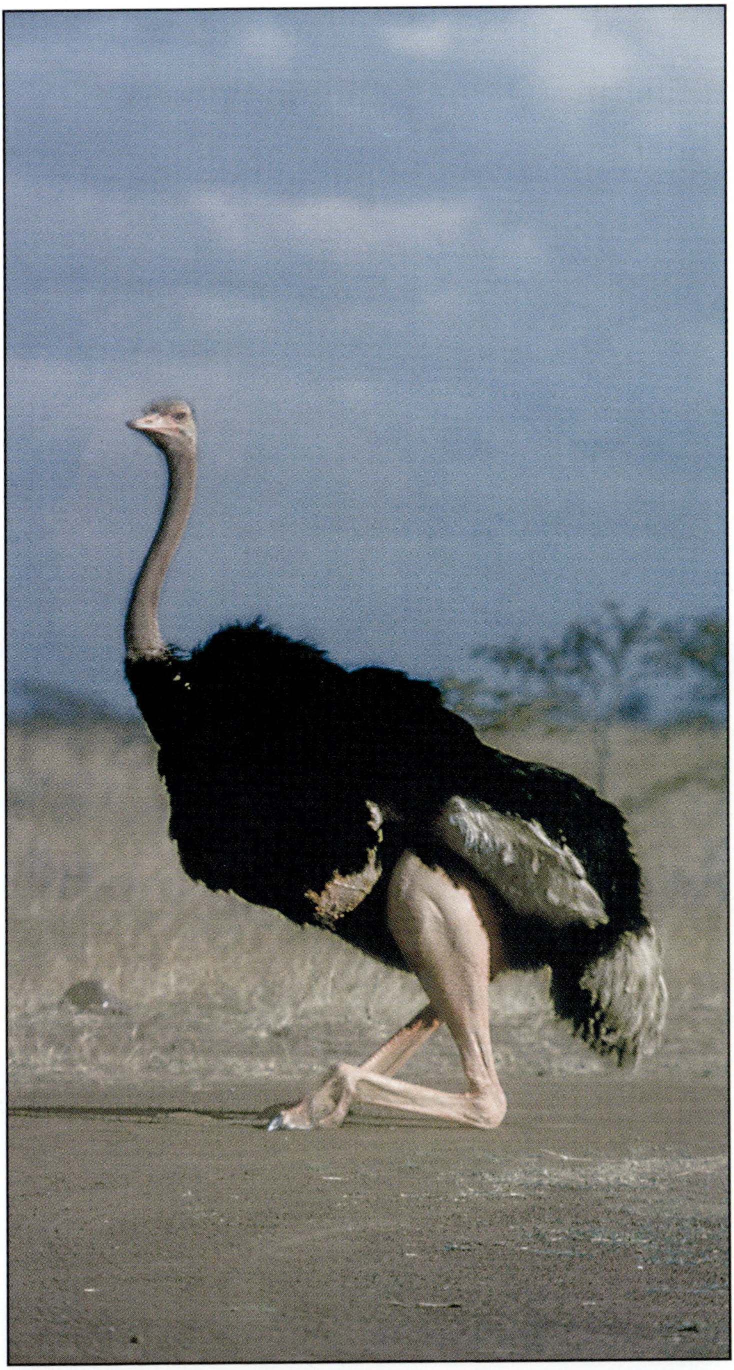

THE LARGEST BIRD

out against the ground just as its mother did when she was sitting on the nest. This makes the chick even harder to see.

How does the father ostrich know to shade the nest of eggs from the hot noon sun? How do the parents know which one should sit on the nest at night and which one during the day? How does an ostrich chick know to flatten itself against the ground when danger appears? These questions must be added to the many unanswered questions about animals that only God, their Creator, can answer.

🐾 Do You Remember?

Circle the correct answer.

1. A pebble is _____.

    (a) a smooth, round stone

    (b) an animal

    (c) a bush

THE LARGEST BIRD

2. To grind up their food, ostriches have
   _____.

   (a) strong back teeth

   (b) pebbles in their stomachs

   (c) sharp toenails

3. The baby ostrich is protected from hawks flying in the sky by_____.

   (a) his parents

   (b) his ability to run fast

   (c) his sandy color

What Do You Think?

1. What ways did God give the ostrich for protecting itself?

2. What has God given you to help you protect yourself?

African Partners

Many kinds of animals live in the jungles and on the plains of Africa. Among these birds and animals are some strange friendships.

You may have wondered how smaller animals protect themselves from the stronger animals. But have you ever wondered how the bigger, stronger animals solve their problems?

Does the crocodile ever have problems? Do you suppose there is any animal brave enough to risk being eaten so he can help the crocodile? After all, a crocodile is not very choosy about what he eats! Birds, deer, monkeys, and even baby elephants are just a few of the foods on the crocodile's menu!

Could a zebra and an ostrich help each other? That may sound like a curious friendship, but they have often saved each other's lives.

When we need help, we can call on our friends. God knew that animals of all kinds would need help, too. Most animals do not trust other animals. For their own protection, God created them that way. But God knew that some animals would have their own special problems and would need special help. For these animals, God created special animal friends.

If God looks after each animal in such a special way, think how well He looks after you. Animals do not ask for God's help, but He constantly gives it to them. Many times we forget to ask for God's help, but He still helps us. Think how much more He could help us if we only took the time to ask Him and to trust Him.

🐾 Do You Remember?
Write the correct answer in the blank.

1. How do most animals feel toward other animals? _they don't trust them_

2. Why did God give special friends to some animals? _to help them with their problems_

3. When does God help us, if He is constantly helping us? _when we take time to ask him for help._

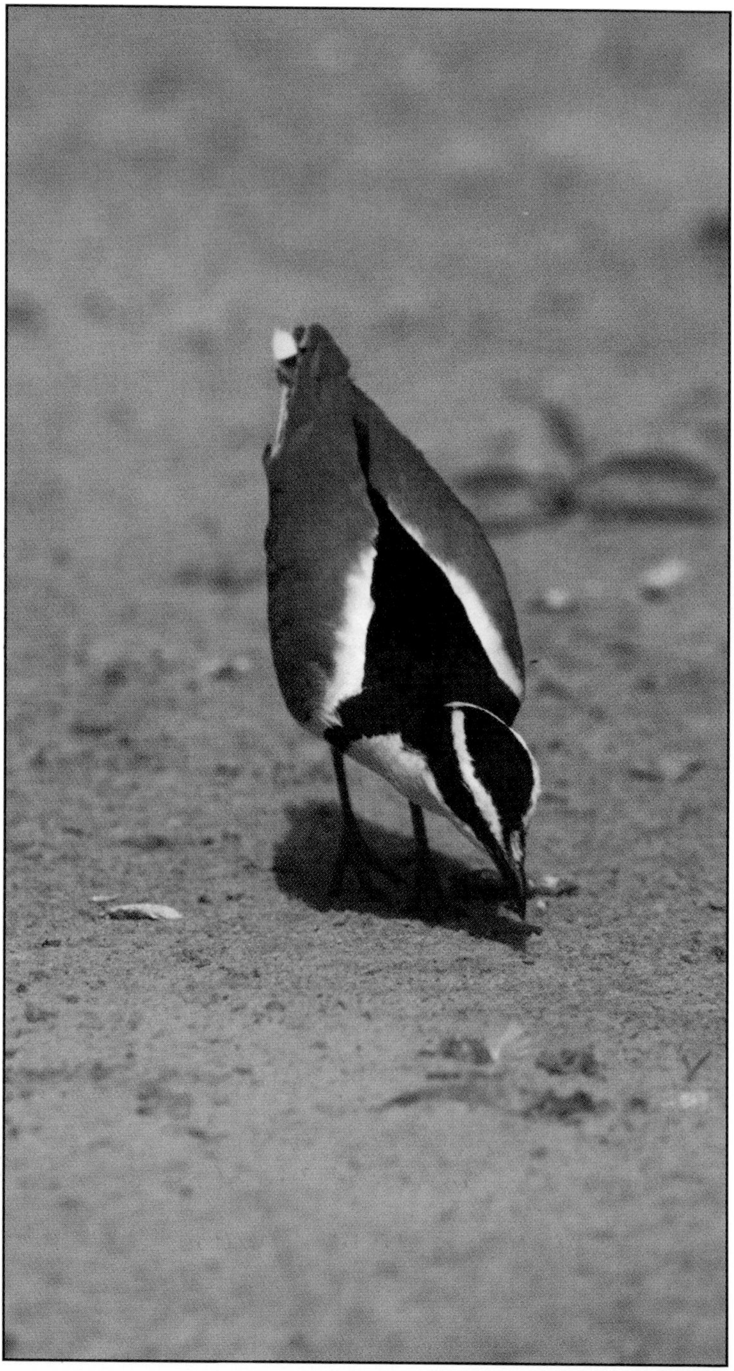

The Crocodile's Dentist

Meet the Crocodile's Friend

If you have ever been to a zoo, perhaps you have gazed from a distance into the huge, toothy mouth of a crocodile. Then, SNAP! Its jaws closed. Woe be to any animal that wanders too near those toothy jaws! That is, every animal but one.

In Africa there is one bird who not only hops all over the crocodile's back, but who also hops right into the crocodile's mouth! Any other small mouthful such as that would be swallowed in a moment as a snack. Yet the powerful jaws of the crocodile stretch open a little wider to allow

> **Words to watch for**
>
> **parasite**—plant or animal that lives on another living thing
> **hide**—tough, thick skin of an animal
> **coursers**—a group of birds that can run very fast

THE CROCODILE'S DENTIST

the bird more room to move around in his mouth.

The bird's name should not surprise you. It is called the crocodile bird. It is also called the Egyptian plover. The crocodile bird is a very pretty gray, black, and white bird. It belongs to a group of birds called *coursers*. Coursers can run better than they can fly. Like other coursers, crocodile birds have only three front toes. They have no hind toes such as birds that perch or fly will have.

Crocodile birds live along the sandy river banks in Africa where crocodiles live. When crocodiles get tired of the water, they crawl up on the bank to rest in the sun. Then the crocodile bird runs from the river bank right onto the crocodile's back. The crocodile eats other birds. Why does the crocodile allow this bird to be so bold? It is because the crocodile bird is a special friend to the crocodile.

THE CROCODILE'S DENTIST

🐾 Do You Remember?

Write the correct answer in the blank.

1. The Egyptian plover is better known as the _crocodile bird_.

2. Coursers are birds that are better at _running_ than flying.

3. Where do crocodile birds live? _in africa._

4. The *bold* crocodile bird is not _afraid_ to walk on the crocodile's back.

🐾 Word Practice

Write the root words.

Egyptian _Egypt_

gazed _gaze_

toothy _tooth_

powerful _power_

194

How the Friends Help Each Other

Many insects and parasites live in most of the African rivers. These insects and parasites attach themselves to other animals in the water. Some even get inside the crocodile's mouth and fasten themselves there. You can imagine how sore the crocodile's mouth would be if there were no way to remove them.

The Crocodile's Dentist

The crocodile bird eats insects and parasites that live on the crocodile's hide. Its job also includes eating the insect pests in the crocodile's mouth and the food caught between its teeth. You might say that this little bird is a dentist for the crocodile.

The crocodile bird also helps the crocodile escape enemies. If the bird senses danger, it will warn the crocodile by giving a shrill cry. Then the crocodile slips back into the safety of the water.

Really, both animals help each other. The crocodile gives the crocodile bird some food. The crocodile bird rids the crocodile of small, bothersome insect pests and parasites.

THE CROCODILE'S DENTIST

🐾 Do You Remember?
Write the correct answer in the blank.

1. How does the crocodile bird help the crocodile (two ways)? _____
   (a) _gets rid of parasites_

   (b) _warns him_____

2. How does the crocodile help his bird friend? _gives him food to eat._

3. Insects and parasites fasten themselves on the crocodile's __hide__ and inside the crocodile's __mouth__.

198

Word Practice

Can you divide these words into syllables?

    in sects   pa ra sites

    cro co dile   bo ther some

What Do You Think?

1. Why doesn't the crocodile eat the crocodile bird?
2. How do your friends help you?

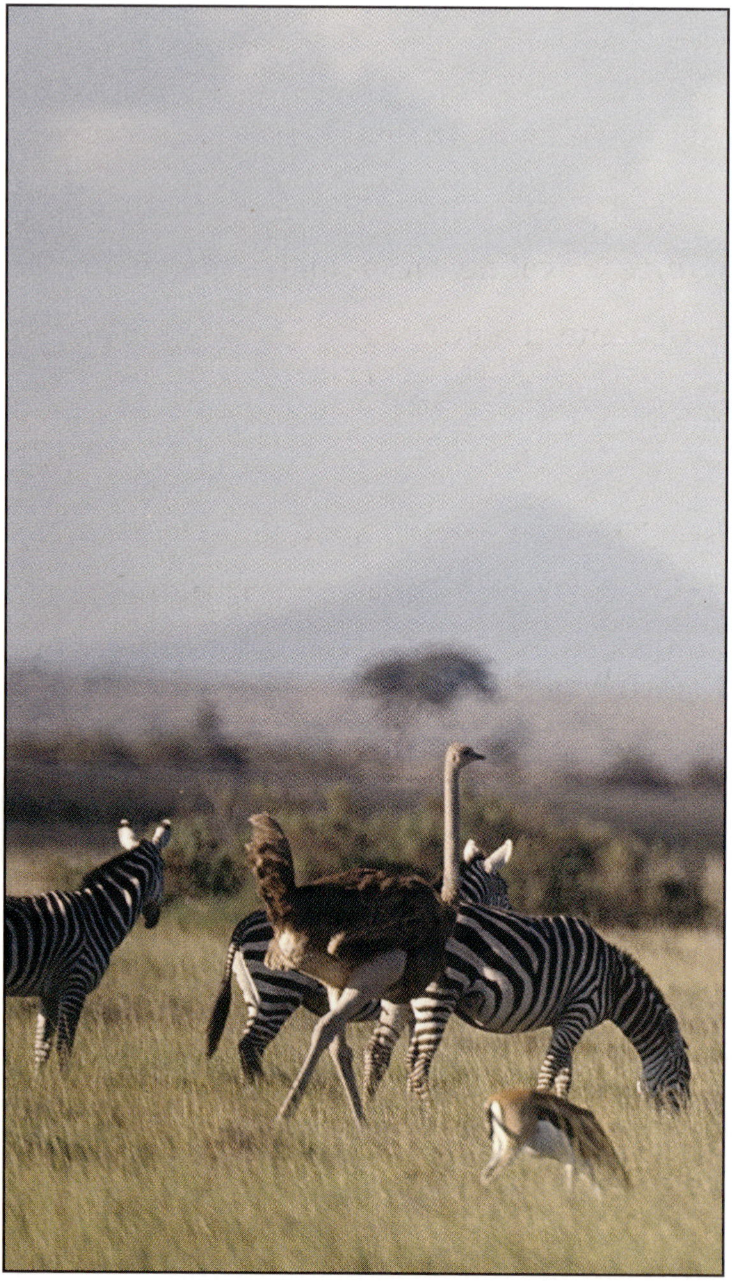

COMPANIONS OF THE OSTRICH

A Two-Way Friendship

On the African plains ostriches can be seen traveling with zebras and sometimes antelopes and gnus. They may seem like strange traveling companions, but the ostrich and the grazing animals greatly benefit from being with each other.

Ostriches are not very choosy about their food. They eat seeds, fruits, and plants as well as any insects and animals that are small enough to be swallowed whole. As the zebras and other grazing animals move

> **Words to watch for**
>
> **hoofs**—the horny coverings that protect the feet of some animals such as horses and cows
> **benefit**—to help; to be kind
> **gnu**—a large African animal that looks like an ox
> **graze**—to eat grass

Companions of the Ostrich

slowly across the plains eating grass, the insects are stirred up. Small animals such as mice and lizards run to escape the hoofs of the animals. This is just what the ostriches are waiting for. They quickly gobble up the scrambling insects and small animals.

But this is not a one-sided friendship. Many times the ostriches have saved the lives of their traveling friends. Most full-grown ostriches are six to eight feet tall. From this height the ostrich's sharp eyes can see danger coming from a far distance. The shorter zebras and other animals cannot see the danger as soon, but when they see the ostrich begin to run, the grazing animals also run.

There are times when the zebras help the ostrich. The ostrich has keen eyes and a better view, but the zebra has a keen sense

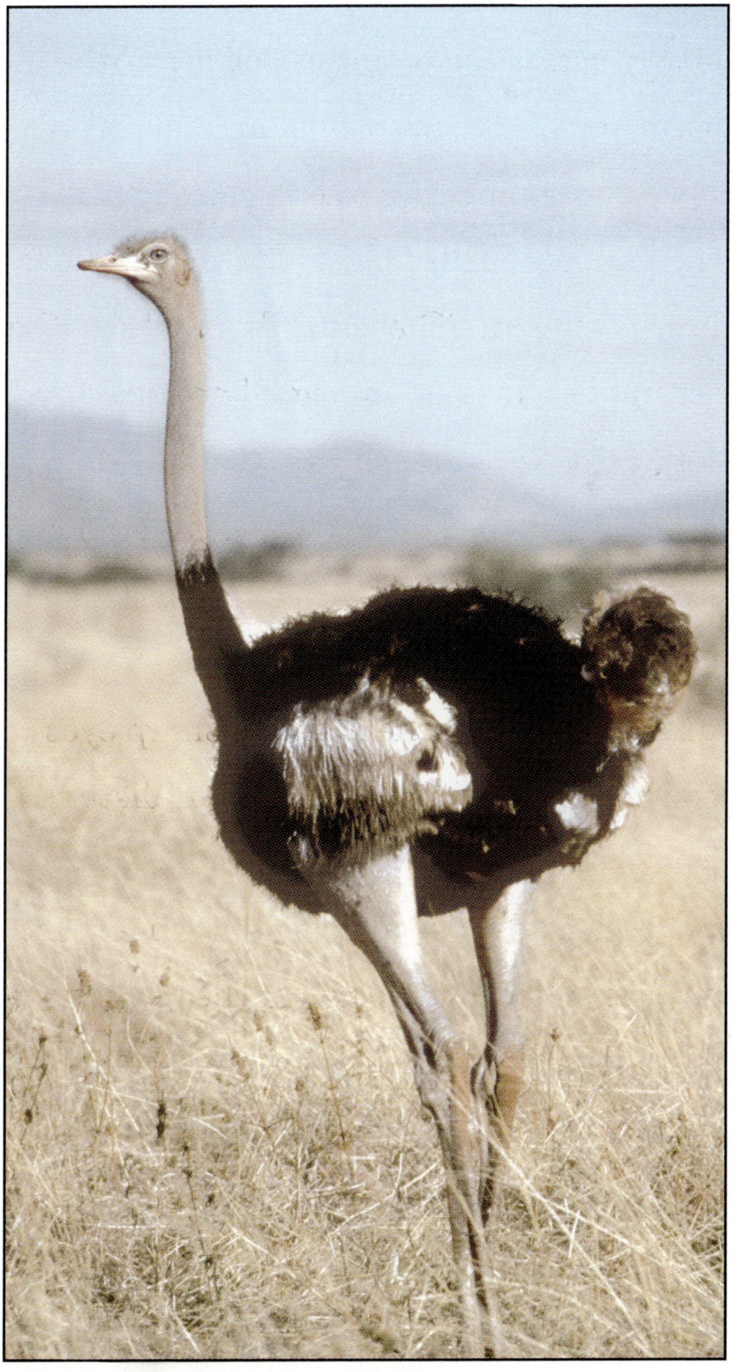

Companions of the Ostrich

of smell. If a lion creeps up on a group of animals under the cover of bushes, neither the zebras nor the ostriches can see it. But the zebra's sense of smell tells him that a lion is near. When a zebra begins running, the ostriches and other animals follow. Running seems to be a danger signal that the other animals do not question.

By traveling with the grazing animals, the ostrich gets better and faster meals. The ostrich is also warned of unseen danger. On the other hand, the grazing animals are warned by the ostrich about dangerous animals that are still far enough away for most of them to escape.

Think of This!

Sometimes troubles come to Christians, too. If God has thought of ways to protect animals and give them a fair chance to escape trouble, don't you think He has planned just as wisely and carefully for you?

The Bible says

"God is faithful, who will not suffer you to be tempted above that ye are able; but will with the temptation also make a way to escape." —*1 Corinthians 10:13*

Companions of the Ostrich

🐾 Do You Remember?

Write the correct answer in the blank.

1. Why can ostriches see danger before zebras do? _the height and sharp eyes_

2. A zebra's sense of _smell_ helps him know danger is near.

3. Why do animals run when they see another animal run? _danger signal_

4. How do grazing animals help ostriches find food? _gets better food and faster meals_

🐾 What Do You Think?

1. Who are the ostrich's friends? How are they different from the ostrich? Is that good?

2. How are your friends different from you? How does their being different help you?

In Conclusion

Think of This!

The stories you have just read all contain true facts about the lives of animals. You may want to study more about them or other kinds of animals. That's good. There are thousands of animals to choose from and thousands of books written about animal life.

Some books that you may read will say that the animal you are reading about came to be the way it is after many years of change. In other words, these books say that animals "just happened" to become the way they are all by themselves. But think for a moment. If the giant panda "just happened," who made sure it was placed in a bamboo jungle? If the panda "just happened" anywhere else, it would starve to death. And if all the zebras had

In Conclusion

had to wait for the ostrich to "just happen," they might all have been eaten up by lions!

Do you want to believe that things "just happened" over many years? People who say this are only making guesses about something no one has ever seen.

On the other hand, we can read from the Bible, "In the beginning, God created...." Which will you believe? Other books, or the Bible?

Do You Remember?
Write the correct answer in the blank.

1. Some people believe that animals _____ to turn out the way they are.

2. The Bible says in Genesis 1:1 that God _____ all the animals.